The Harp in Distant Healing

for individuals, animals,
nature spirits & earth healing

Daniel Perret

What you learn to do at a distance,
can improve what you do for somebody present.

The use of musical instruments to help nature and the elementals was apparently known in 16th century Sussex, by people in connection with the contemporary Swiss alchemist and medical doctor Paracelsus. It was known and used in Ancient Egypt and by the Celts on the continent before this. This shows that the practice is rare, possibly because of a number of conditions having to come together for it to work. (see page 31)

I have received essential parts of this text and the above text from a group of spirit beings I call the 'Harp Distant Healing Think Tank'. To them go all my thanks. Thanks to Marie for correcting my English.

© 2020 Daniel Perret
Edition: BoD - Books on Demand GmbH
12/14 rond-point des Champs Elysées
75008 Paris, France
Imprimé par BoD - Books on Demand GmbH
Norderstedt, Allemagne

ISBN 9782322208623
Dépôt légal : May 2020

Table of Content

Distant Healing with the harp, like prayer, is very simple.
Yet to become simple the road is sometimes long.

What does the harp transmit in distant healing?
The absent receiver doesn't see you, doesn't hear you, usually can't talk to you, or touch you. Distant healing operates in the invisible realm of feeling. Anything that could otherwise impress the receiver does not operate anymore.

Preface

This is a collection of texts previously published either as part of my books or on my website for free downloading. I decided to group them together for those who prefer to hold a paper version in their hands.

My thanks go to Alix Colin and the International Harp Therapy Program who invited me in summer 2019 to teach in Belgium and Holland. This brought about, already during the preparation of those courses, an unexpected contact to a new think tank of spirit beings: The Harp Distant Healing Think Tank. In spring 2019 I also discovered, probably with the hint of that think tank, the energy fields around my harps and what they meant.

I have been studying, researching, and teaching Spiritual Healing and distant healing for 40 years. I bought my first harp, a Salvi pedal harp, in 1981. I have also been sending healing prayers for some years now to nature spirits that were asking. In spring 2019 they began to tell me that they also wanted me to play the harp for them as part of distant healing. Each time I could see on an energy level, that their request was satisfied by my harp playing.

The Think Tank remains with a visible energy pattern – a 315° segment - around my quartz crystal since spring 2019, signaling that they are continuously supporting this research and writing about Distant Healing with the Harp.

Introduction

There is a deep link between the harp and the divine field. Most harpists and people can feel this to be true. This is usually felt in the heart area, which by nature is a link to the spiritual dimension, either to our timeless soul or to the divine field.

I have come to understand, with the help of the Think Tank, that all string instruments with resonating strings, have a distant healing potential comparable to harps: sitar, hammered dulcimer, Austrian or Bavarian zithers, monochords, and suchlike.

Other musical instruments of course do have their beauty and unique ways to spread joy and healing, yet, what I describe here seems unique to these types of string instruments.

Distant Healing with or without the harp is not very complicated. You just need to have a feeling for doing it. There are few other skills on the harp requested than playing with your feelings. Yet, what feelings really are is a vast subject and certainly worth exploring, because feelings are different from good intentions.

The Harp in distant Healing part 1

Little did I know all those years ago when I labelled my work « Music & Energy » how these two words would be the guideline of my research and come together today so beautifully. It was actually my teacher Bob Moore who used these two words together in the foreword he wrote for my first book: « Music – The feeling way ». The 'feeling way' catches the essence of how to explore the deeper aspects of both music and energy. Both create an opening to a vastness that words alone cannot describe.

When I met my teacher, I knew instantly that I had to completely change my music. This led me to buy my concert harp. I also instinctively knew that I could not learn to play the harp in a classical or traditional way. I only ever had one harp lesson in Zurich with a great lady harpist called Emmy Hürlimann. She taught me the essential: how to place my fingers and how to change a string on the instrument. You need to know how to tie a special knot with the bass strings. It is as if she knew she would not see me again and that she had to teach me the basics there and then. I just knew that I could not study the harp through classical music or through reading notes.

This 'feeling' approach to music was not new to me as I had by then spent ten years learning various traditional types of music orally, just by listening and watching. I had been deeply moved by the humility and generosity of traditional folk musicians such as my Irish pipe teacher Willie Reynolds who lived near Athlone. I also saw these same qualities in Appalachian old-time music as played by the New Lost City Ramblers or the Carter Family. I had met a great humanness with those musicians, a naturalness, and a vast respect. Bob Moore himself was Irish and had this same quality.

In 2019 the two strands 'Music and Energy' merged in a completely unexpected way. I was shown that one could send **distant healing by playing the harp**. I have been teaching trainings in the healing aspects of music and sound for many years so I was not unfamiliar with the issue. Yet, what was revealed to me took me entirely by surprise.

It took me many years to trust 'my' style on the concert harp as I did and could not copy anybody. Completing a classical or traditional training would give you a type of security of belonging to a musical 'tribe'. Not belonging in that way to any particular style made me feel at times insecure about where I was going with my harp playing. Yet, I persevered because I began to deeply love the beautiful sound of the harp; particularly its deep notes and the multitudes of harmonics that spread out after plucking each string. I never got into stopping the strings with the flat of my hand as many harpists do. For me this felt like killing the sound. I rather felt drawn to let the harp sing naturally.

Independently from my harp playing I have been sending daily **distant healing** for many years now. This involves a short meditation period where I focus on a list of names, beings and places on earth that require healing. People normally need to ask to be included.

In recent years my interest in healing has developed more and more in the direction of including **nature and nature spirits** of all kinds. I had not been looking for that at all. They came to me in the form of energy lines converging towards a quartz crystal that incidentally was placed

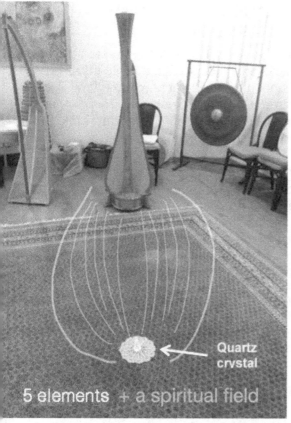

5 elements + a spiritual field

Quartz crystal

before me on the floor of our meditation room. Fortunately, I had learned how to sense energy with my teacher. I am teaching this in my courses on spiritual healing so I saw that my students could also sense the energy lines that showed at the crystal. They could also observe how all these lines disappeared after sending distant healing.

Energy fields around the harp

In early 2019 I noticed several energy fields enveloping the harp. I could distinctly make out six energy fields for the five elements and a spiritual energy field. I will come back to that. One day I became curious to see whether there were even more energy fields further out around the harp.

I then discovered two more energy fields around it. One appeared to be an astral/mental field reaching up to about four meters away from the harp. Then another field started that is linked to a Seraphim. All this needs to be explained.

Lately during distant healing another energy signature appeared around the crystal. It is a 315° segment. Surprisingly enough it seems

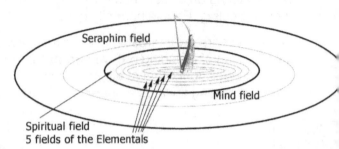

to be linked to other harpists in the world who are interested by the deeper aspects of the harp. As I had just started to write these lines, this seemed to explain the appearance of that new signature. This made me feel that there was something to be shared. This connection seems to link to a kind of invisible **Harp Distant Healing Think Tank** or a group of souls and beings researching into the healing qualities of harp playing. I believe that every harpist interested in this subject potentially has access to it and is feeding their understanding (perhaps unconsciously) into that pool of information. Some spirit beings like Saint Cecilia *the patron saint of musicians* are part of it, as well as a being from Vega that is in the constellation of stars called Lyra. Lyra relates to the Greek myth of Orpheus and the healing qualities of his harp playing. Although some of this information may seem slightly far out, they link to some myths that have a meaning in our context.

Music as well as energy are both normally invisible yet both have their own distinct language with its own particular alphabet. Both are essentially a means of communication not just between people but also in a larger sense with intelligent beings, visible or invisible.

I studied Spiritual Healing with Bob Moore my Irish teacher for twenty years and to a certain extent I learned to perceive and decipher **the language of energy.** The basic symbols of energy are: point, line, cross/square, circle, and triangle. You find them both in landscapes and with human energy fields for instance.

The way of **perceiving energy** can be different for each person. This has mainly to do with the individual faculties that we have brought with us right from birth. When we are able to transform 'gross' emotional issues we get easier access to faculties like clairaudience, clairvoyance, higher sense of touch, etc. The latter is mostly my way of perceiving energy and I often sense it as columns of energy or directly with my hands. Through using my Hartmann antenna, I can then ask what or who this energy column is.

When energy phenomenon first started to draw my attention around the **quartz crystal** in our meditation room, I noticed lines converging towards it. I had no clue at first why they appeared and what they meant. The first line stayed for days, so I thought I'd follow it to see if it led to something. It brought me to a water spirit, also called an *undine* that was about 20 meters outside our house. Having learned how to use a small Hartmann antenna (a small type of dowsing rod) to ask questions giving a yes or no answer, I discovered that the *undine* wanted to tell me something. She told me that I had written something wrong in my last book that I needed to correct. I had written that the spirit of our valley was situated at the first water source about 300 meters below our house. The *undine* said that this was not correct, because her well, in the field next to our house was the first or highest source of the valley. When I promised to correct this, she left and the line disappeared. I learned a major lesson: even a small injustice creates disharmony and thus an unbalance.

Since then I have had hundreds of different types of spirit beings coming to the crystal who need some sort of help or action on my part. In the majority of cases I had no idea how to help them other than by saying a prayer. Recently spirit beings told me I could do the same with playing the harp for a specific request and being. Each time the lines disappeared and any other people in the room could easily detect this for themselves.

I have written lengthily about these encounters in my recent book on Earth Healing (French and German editions only, for the moment, but also some information on my website in English).

I include the following diagram that may be of help to you. It shows the precision with which these invisible beings manifest themselves.
The center point in the drawing is the quartz crystal. The lines show the section of the circle between 0° and the line.

Except the first type of lines that are coming from Devas and small elementals like the *undine*, all other signatures were segments of a circle with precise angles, each type of segment announcing the presence of a specific type of being needing distant healing.
Devas are beings that

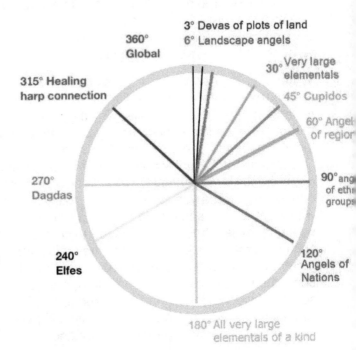

- 360° Global
- 3° Devas of plots of land
- 6° Landscape angels
- 30° Very large elementals
- 45° Cupidos
- 60° Angel of region
- 90° ang of eth groups
- 315° Healing harp connection
- 270° Dagdas
- 240° Elfes
- 120° Angels of Nations
- 180° All very large elementals of a kind

belong to their own Deva hierarchy. They are neither nature spirits in the strict sense of the term nor do they belong to the angelic hierarchy. Devas build the connecting link between nature spirits (elementals) and angels.

Although they often quite willingly gave me information about who and where they were and the type of problem that they were coming with, this became simpler as time went by. They mostly just communicate their presence and request for harp healing and the lines always disappear right after my harp playing. In recent months I use a **global**

healing approach when contacting the crystal in distant healing; I include all the beings, problems and geographic areas that are around the crystal on that day. All of this can also be done without a crystal. I feel that the energy lines also come directly to my own energy field around me. It is just that the crystal allows you to sense and see it in front of me.

The different energy signatures around the crystal took about two years to show themselves one after the other. I worked for example for about two months almost exclusively with regional angels when they appeared. Each one showed me the area of Europe they were covering.

Devas: an intermediary people between elementals and the angel hierarchy. We find a Deva for each plot of land, each tree, group of plants in a garden e.g.; they are directing the myriads of elementals.

Landscape Angels: They are looking after a circular area of a ray of 1 km, directing the Devas. They are part of the angel hierarchy that includes angels of larger areas (50 km ray), of nations and continents.

Elementals: On the smallest scale they are the gnomes (earth), undines (water), salamanders (fire), and sylphs (air). They are imbedded in a hierarchy reaching up to medium, large, and very large elementals that cover most of a country.

This of course brings up a number of **obvious questions**:
Who is it that helps them come to the crystal? How does that come about? How can I trust what the lines and the Hartmann antenna bring as answers? Who is actually answering? How does distant healing and more specifically distant harp healing operate? What does it really contribute and on what level? Is anyone capable of contributing to distant healing? Can any musical instrument do this? Is there anything particular about harps and healing? What and how should we play for any request?

My sources

I should start by presenting the think tank of spirit beings I have been working with during the last five years. I call them 'C' for collegium of spirits. I have written several books together with them. They are my main source. This group of spirits has 12 members in their inner and permanent circle and a number of specialists they can draw upon when needed. They are anchored in Rocamadour, a famous pilgrimage place in SW France. They started operating 1000 years ago under the initiative of Saint Amadour and the Deva Queen of the SW of France. I have described who they are in my book on 'Earth healing'. (only German and French editions for the moment).

Since spring 2019 I came in contact with the Harp Distant Healing Think Tank. They are guiding the understanding on this particular subject.

Then there are the various nature spirits themselves coming with their individual requests.

The crystal is in itself a transmitter and has a particular being - a *Dagda* - connected to it. Dagdas come from the Celtic Irish tradition and are related to Indian and Tibetan Dakinis. They seem to be experts on crystals and nature spirits of all kind.

Then there is a new type of elementary beings called elementary beings of the fifth type. Some also call them 'Christic' elementals. The four others are the elementals of earth, water, fire, and air. These beings of the 5th type have come into existence in recent years to encourage a co-operation between humans and nature spirits. [7]

I occasionally ask other spirit beings, including beings from the angelic realm, when I need to know something that only they could know.

Methodology

Invisible beings communicate with us essentially through energy. In some cases, they are channeled directly through a medium. While their language is precise, our interpretation of what we perceive may be less so. How can we verify who we are dealing with and whether we understand them correctly? We need to use our common sense: is the information that they share uplifting, coherent, consistent, reasonably stable over a period and without contradictions? Do they bring us a better understanding of spiritual dimensions? Is the information raising our consciousness? Does the information bring us anything new and worthwhile for individuals or society? Simply being extraordinary is not enough. Is our interpretation biased by group pressure, to please other people e.g.? Does the source lend itself to be checked out, through asking them directly or through other means of perception like clairvoyance, other practitioners, etc.?

The harp

It seems to me that there is more to the connection between **harps and angels** than we might at first think. I am quite reluctant to venture into what we may consider to be esoteric. I always feel a need to bring things into an accessible way of understanding. However, the co-operation with the 'think tank C' obviously brings us insights from beyond our everyday understanding. I feel they want to underline how much we contribute and mean to them. I have observed that each of my musical instruments

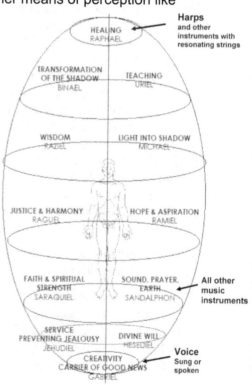

HEALING
RAPHAEL

Harps and other instruments with resonating strings

TRANSFORMATION OF THE SHADOW
BINAEL

TEACHING
URIEL

WISDOM
RAZIEL

LIGHT INTO SHADOW
MICHAEL

JUSTICE & HARMONY
RAGUEL

HOPE & ASPIRATION
RAMIEL

FAITH & SPIRITUAL STRENGTH
SARAQUIEL

SOUND, PRAYER, EARTH
SANDALPHON

All other music instruments

SERVICE PREVENTING JEALOUSY
JEHUDIEL

DIVINE WILL
HESEDIEL

CREATIVITY CARRIER OF GOOD NEWS
GABRIEL

Voice
Sung or spoken

seems to have an invisible being connected with it and I wanted to know by whom these beings and instruments were looked after in the spirit world. C had shown me the connection between the twelve archangels, their tasks, and the human chakras. I had understood that Sandalphon was taking care of musical instruments. This scheme recently led me to ask which of the twelve archangels was looking after harps. C told me it was **Archangel Raphael** whose field of action is **healing**. They then said that all other instruments were attributed to Sandalphon. The voice, in speech or singing, was linked to Archangel Gabriel, the *bringer of good news*, as we know from the Bible. I feel that noticing differences brings awareness into an area that until then had only been grossly perceived.

This distinction between the three sources of sound sets the harp apart into a particular healing aspect. The reason, I feel, is its unique display of harmonics that is already noticeable when playing a single note. It is this abundant presence of harmonics in harp playing which might bring the resulting sound closest to the music of the (angelic) spheres. The presence of **a Seraphim related energy layer** around the harp adds onto the unique quality of harps. I need to qualify this last statement. As far as I understand, the four ethers and the spiritual energy field near the harp are linked directly to the instrument itself. This gives the harp a natural healing power towards the beings of the four ethers and that includes nature spirits and elementals. The anthroposophical understanding explains that, due to earlier phases of evolution of planet earth, the qualities of harmony and wisdom are inbuilt in nature. Perhaps this is the reason why the harmony of music resonates especially well with nature spirits.

The **four ethers** are: chemical or sound ether, light ether, life ether and reflector or warmth ether.

The **astral/mental field** around a harp reflects the level of consciousness of the harpist and thus the potential impact that the harpist has on those levels. This particular field is NOT just the personal aura of the harpist but the blend that the musician has built up with and around their harp in that level.

The presence of a **Seraphim layer** means that something special is most likely taking place during harp playing. Seraphim are high angels of light and fire. They are igniters of souls, bringing the 'spark' or the (holy) spirit.

Observing these different energy layers around a harp may encourage us to be grateful and open to learning more about the mystery of the harp. This can encourage us to go even further in the exploration of the potential of the harp and of our own path of development.

I always emphasize that the quality of each sound healing needs to take into consideration at least **five factors**: 1. The quality of the instrument, 2. The musical elements used (loudness, musical mode, key, tuning, etc.), 3. The receptivity of the receiver, 4. The level of consciousness the music healer is using, 5. The energies of the place and time of day and year.

Choosing to do a sound healing treatment with an impressive instrument for instance and neglecting the other aspects would not work as this would only include one of the five factors.

How can a musician can raise their **level of consciousness?** This is a fascinating question that I devote most of my teaching to and which involves personal transformation work and is connected to learning about energy. I have written extensively about this in previous books.

What kind of playing is conducive for distant harp healing?
This is a big question that I do not necessarily have a final answer to. However, it is clear that a number of aspects are absent in distant harp healing as there is no direct human contact (words, visual, etc.), no direct acoustic sound impact, no melodic perception, no perceived technical skills. What remains are more subtle forms of energy transmission that transcend both time and space. What are they?

I have taught and written extensively about the **five elements** earth, water, fire, air, and space determining the inner quality of a piece of music (see p 46). They each relate to a chakra or body zone and to a specific set of emotions that we can learn to transform. You can download for free both books and chapters about this from my website. Let me summarize some aspects of it here. **Space** *(thyroid chakra)* obviously brings the quality of silence and space to one's music. It is seldom found enough in music. The element of *air (chest area, heart chakra)* brings the quality of generosity, the harmonic structure, the melodic aspect with its wide swoops reminding us of the flight of birds. With **fire** *(solar plexus)* we get the fiery and dynamic loudness aspect, the warmth. **Water** *(hara)* is linked to lively rhythms, that includes variations in rhythms, both slowing and accelerations. The element of **earth** *(root chakra, legs, and feet)* gives us a sense of stability and a fundamental structure in music including the pulsation or a drone effect.

We also have an immense variety of **musical modes** that reach well beyond the 7 well-known church modes: Phrygian, Mixolydian, Lydian, Dorian modes etc. The harp, particularly the pedal harp, lends itself beautifully to exploring over a hundred musical modes, including numerous pentatonic and hexatonic modes. It would require the type of understanding that there is in Indian music to be able to value and approach all the intervals in order to access the wealth of possibilities of each mode, even those that at first may sound odd or too unusual. It is worth exploring each of the seven modes offered by any musical scale, as each note in the scale can be used as the fundamental note. A number of modes may not lend themselves to a full-scale musical development but they often bring some progression of intervals that can prove very valuable in order to contact specific inspirational spaces.

Here is an example of the well-known **melodic minor** with its sequence of intervals 1212222. The numbers correspond to the semitones between one note and the next in the scale. Therefore they always add up to 12. Most of these scales contain more than one mode. The number 1 stands for a small second, the number 2 for the large second. This notation is tonality neutral, that is it can be started on any of the twelve notes of the octave. Some of the notes of that mode lend themselves more easily to be a fundamental than others. For the numerous modes see my book 'Music – The feeling Way' downloadable for free on my website. Here some pentatonic scales from it and the feeling they may convey:

18   5-note-scales - pentatonic music

1)	22332	light
2)	23223	island, clarity, calm, joy
3)	14223	autumn, swirl in the air
4)	41223	crystal
5)	14232	fairy tale, multi-coloured
6)	41232	space, wide open landscape, cathedral
7)	14322	flight of a bird
8)	41322	waiting, suspense
9)	12432	morning
10)	23421	rainbow
11)	14214	crimson, Egypt, aeolian
12)	41241	Balinese, brass, penetrative, light, bell
13)	33114	vortex, spiralling
14)	21225	deep forest, dark, mysterious
15)	22125	cradle song, light, clear
16)	32331	blues
17)	12144	snake
18)	5 times 2,4 notes = slendro (Bali)	

Many of these pentatonic scales have more than one useful mode, which again depends on the note used as the basic one. None of these scales or modes are contained in any of the sixteen other pentatonic scales. For instance, the second one, the most widely spread, does have 5 modes:

2a)	23223	island, clarity, calm, joy
2b)	32232	Andes, Greece
2c)	22323	Chinese
2d)	23232	Mongolian
2e)	32322	Japanese, spring, joy

Some hexatonic / 6 note scales

221232	joy, clarity, spring, sun
221223	major scale without 7th. has got a Celtic feeling about it.
211323	this basically pentatonic scale gives us the choice between a major and a minor version.
212223	seems to me to be a scale that comes from ancient European times. it is a melodic minor without its 7th.
122214	...

When I bought my concert harp, I explored its modal possibilities by drawing the atmosphere I felt from each mode.

heptatonic / 7 note scales

2212221	a straight road, clarity, strength, will, no ambiguity, male, determined. **Ionian mode.**
2122212	**Dorian mode.** evokes noble feelings as well as an opening towards an inner world.
1222122	**Phrygian mode.** 'religious'. from suffering to its transformation. Poetic, calm, resting in itself.
2221221	**Lydian mode.** a bit airy, elevating towards a lighter space. fine and delicate. not resting in itself.
2212212	**Mixolydian mode.** melodious, warm.
2122122	**Aeolian mode.** 'pure minor'. very pure and fine mode. can evoke the feeling of the colour rose pink.
1221222	**Locrian mode.** closed in the lower notes, wider in the upper ones, disturbing feeling. tension.
2122221	**melodic minor**. try modes starting from the 2nd, 4th and 5th note.
2122131	**harmonic minor**. a generous feeling about this scale, very moving.

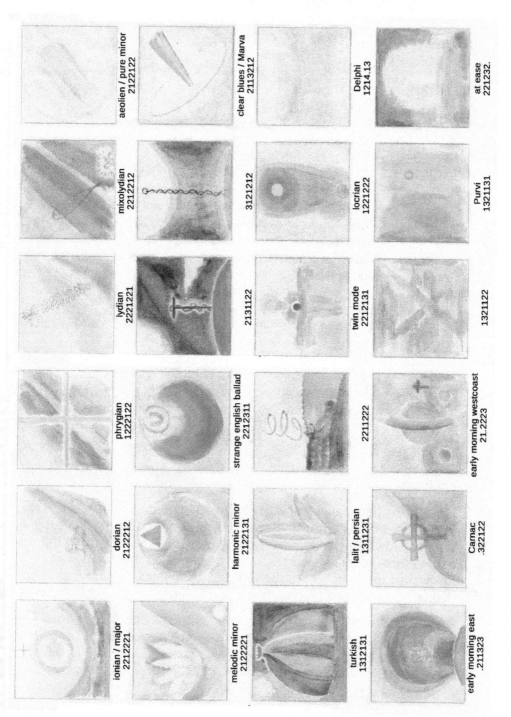

aeolien / pure minor
2122122

clear blues / Marva
211321 2

Delphi
1214.13

at ease
221232.

mixolydian
2212212

3121212

locrian
1221222

Purvi
1321131

lydian
2221221

2131122

twin mode
2212131

1321122

phrygian
1222122

strange english ballad
2212311

2211222

early morning westcoast
21.2223

dorian
2122212

harmonic minor
2122131

lalit / persian
1311231

Carnac
.322122

ionian / major
2212221

melodic minor
2122221

turkish
1312131

early morning east
.211323

Daniel Perret – The Harp in Distant Healing

2113212	**'clear blues'**. try especially the mode starting on the 5th note.
1312131	brings forward feelings of **Turkish and Balkan** spaces. dance.
1311231	a **Persian** feeling about it
2212311	all seems to happen between the normal 7th and the diminished 7th (see intervals). no 6th. the normal 7th will most likely be omitted while descending the scale and used instead of the diminished 7th while going up the scale.
2212131	**'twin mode'**. we again meet the major scale with a diminished 6th this time. Resulting in a major scale in its lower notes and having a 'minor' feeling in its upper notes. devotional, prayer, strength.
1312212	a mode of the 'twin mode'. very melodious and joyous, with a 'minor' feeling to it.
1321122	an **'Arabic'** feeling to it. It evokes the atmosphere around midnight and just before. The interval 'tritonus' asks for some work towards the light (that we would have for free with the normal 5th. the tritonus being a diminished 5th). you might want to use the tritonus only when moving up the scale.
1312221	
1212132	

I find this richness invaluable for finding and adapting the appropriate feeling opening to any requested unusual space or being. It is essential for me in my harp playing to feel **total freedom** in choosing all the parameters: tonality, mode, level of playing, etc. I frequently feel I have to adapt notes in a mode whilst playing, leading immediately of course to a change of mode, feeling and energy.

A third register of musical quality, after elements and modes, may come from the **source of inspiration** we get in touch with. There is not much we can do about that. Inspiration comes like a gust of wind comparable to sudden intuitions or insights. I have quite extensively explored and written about the different sources and spheres of inspiration together with C. See my website or more so in my book 'Creating Divine Art – the source of inspiration'. [5]

This is an extremely interesting subject as soon as we can accept the possibly that our thoughts and feelings are not generated solely within us. I distinguish between three types of inspiration: mental concepts, emotions or feelings, and the divine field. The lower half of the astral and the mental inspiration levels are impregnated by the ego, the upper half being free from that influence.

What concerns us as musicians is **how much our ego is interfering** in the transposition of pure inspirations into our musical expression. Obviously if our playing is largely dictated by our own sense of inferiority or inner restlessness, to name only two possible obstacles, then our music will be affected and the inspiration that could flow into our expression will be extremely limited. It is through personal transformation work that we can raise our level of consciousness and frequency. This will largely determine which levels of beings and inspiration we can contact. I find it more helpful and interesting to focus on this inner work than focus on the dexterity of our fingers or on any acrobatic and impressive playing on the harp.

A piece of music unfolds over several minutes and during that time the levels of inspiration and manifestation often change.

Here is an example of a piece of choir music in the graph below which shows the various levels the inspiration that the composition came from. The level of interpretation is comparatively high. We rarely consider that the subtle qualities of such a recording can reach back to the beings that have inspired it. Those spirit beings enjoy a high level of interpretation just as much as the worldly audience. A complete interplay always takes place between the physical and non-physical levels. We may not understand much about these spheres of inspiration, yet they open a window towards a new outlook that we will gradually learn to appreciate much more than by simply labeling them as the divine field, God or the universe.

In my understanding we also need to differentiate between different **levels of conception in music**. One level is not better than another but simply fulfills a different purpose. Just as much as there are the (physical-acoustic) sounds of the letters of the alphabet, then on the next level the linguistic meaning of each letters, then the Egyptian hieroglyphs or Chinese pictograms, and ultimately the feeling of the sounds.

„Es ist ein Ros entsprungen"

Arrangement Bernat Vivancos, Album 'In Montibus Sanctis'
Degré de manifestation 97 % (composition) / interprétation 99 % - les deux restent constant durant tout le morceau

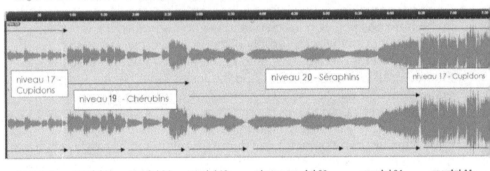

mental 15	mental 11	mental 24	mental 18	niveau mental 22	mental 24	mental 11
ange de la nation	coopération avec des êtres non-physiques	dévotion	alignement et équilibre énergétique	développement spirituel	dévotion	coopération av des êtres non-physiques

In music you find comparable **levels of conceptualization**. We may have first (1) the sounds themselves, then (2) drone and trance music. We have next (3) the basic melodic and rhythmical music used in dance, pop, or classical music (usually 4 beats/3 to 4 chords). On the next level (4) we may find music with simultaneous multiple layers of composition. Then (5) freely improvised and thus highly complex and feeling music. Then (6) simply felt sounds and possibly next (7) the music of the spheres, not within our reach. Each of these levels leads us into a completely different state of mind. Level 3 is brilliant for festive activity. Level 6 may be very useful in helping somebody prepare for 'the great transition' and the letting go that we call the death process. Level 3 obviously tends to bring more fun and joy.

Levels 5 and 6 may open us to deeper aspects of feelings, etc. (see also page 97)

In my experience playing the harp with feeling rather than concepts allows healing energy to flow through us. You can of course play any type of music with feeling. It is very helpful to be aware of limiting concepts that we may subconsciously hold onto and free ourselves from them so that we can be more open when we play. Our playing would very likely need to be improvised, as we can see from the levels of music concepts. It means playing from an inner feeling and not from wanting to impress others. When we can balance the five elements within us we have a better access to the freedom and openness needed to improvise.

There are a number of **other parameters** you might wish to consider in order to develop a deeper feeling contact. Although the harp does not easily lend itself to changing tonal systems, it is very worthwhile exploring some of them. I feel that each tonal system possesses a completely different mental framework or way of thinking: the overtone scale, the undertone scale, also the 'Schlesinger' or Aulos scale, the Balinese slendro system, the solfeggio scale, the random 'flower pot scale'. Another parameter is to be aware of whether you feel like playing at a particular time or place at all or not. Forcing yourself to do something you do not feel for cuts you off from your feelings.

The question of the 432 Hz for the A
This is a debate that never seems to end. However, the solution is simple. When you want to play with others whose instruments can only play in 440 you adapt. If you can choose, follow your feelings. There are good arguments for 432 but if you cannot feel the difference and feel better with 440, don't make it a problem

How does distant healing actually operate?
This question is similar to asking how does prayer work?
The Think Tank underlines that becoming aware of the feeling in each interval, the space between two notes, leads us into the subtle aspects of the harp's potential. A number of scientific researches show that

prayer and distant healing have a considerable effect. Quantum physics tells us that two related cells stay connected even when separated over very long distances, even over thousands of kilometers. The ancient saying "all is connected" reflects the same understanding. I believe our mental and spiritual energy fields know no physical distance. There is an enormous amount to discover about the potential of our upper mental energy field. The human aura includes, at some distance from the physical body, layers that are connected to the whole planet and even one layer that connects to the universe. These layers can be felt around another person starting at 9 meters away from the body and the other at approximately 90 meters from the body.

Both prayer and distant healing work best once we have eliminated our own doubts or feelings of inferiority/superiority. Eliminating them requires us first of all to become aware of them. Our feelings are of paramount importance in this.

We need to understand **the different levels of feelings**. Starting at the densest level we have our *painful emotions* such as anger, jealousy, hate, depression, etc. They belong to what is known as the lower astral. The upper astral contains the transformed emotions that then become *feelings*, like joy, compassion, etc. Beyond the astral we come to the *refined or subtle feelings*. They are the tools of perception and discernment involved in observing the divine field or finer fields of energy. They allow us to become aware of phenomena difficult to describe with words yet perfectly discernable through our subtle feelings.

Is there anything specific about distant healing with the harp?
With the person present for healing, you work with the direct impact of the sound and your human presence as the harpist. All the five factors play a role. Harp playing for healing can operate on a number of levels, from pleasant, comforting to deeply moving and working on subtle levels. On the subtle level the harp has a particular potential. What you can do with the harp at a distance, you can also do for somebody present. Inversely this is not necessarily the case. It depends on the level you are working on. Spiritual healing can operate on different

levels but would tend to use higher levels of consciousness. We can learn to do that.

We need to understand what we are aiming for and on what level we are able to contribute healing in a particular situation? We need to clearly see our true motivation and limits. I often underline the **three permanent 'inner building sites'** involved: 1) inner transformation work on ourselves, 2) developing a deeper contact with the Divine and 3) deepening our grounding or contact with Mother Earth - that is part of our on-going work as long as we are on earth. I emphasize: Things come to us when we are ready. The path is part of the learning we are here for. There is no short cut, and no meaning in a short cut. Any forcing comes from an ego level, from fear and a rejection of oneself.

When we use **distant healing with the harp**, we are likely to get into quite a different mindset. When the recipient is not present or indeed invisible, in the case of nature spirits in a large sense of the word, our intellect is best left completely aside. Holding onto concepts may prove vain, unreal, and largely based on ego. So, what then comes into operation? What intelligence takes over?

In my experience of sending distant healing to numerous invisible beings of all kinds I came to the conclusion that my understanding was and likely will remain very limited. I see myself as being similar to an old-time telephone switchboard operator. There are incoming calls or requests and specialists are needed to respond to the request. I see my role in distant healing as being a link person or the one who has a role to play in establishing connections. I do not really know from whom the incoming call is coming nor do I know who the requested specialist actually is. We don't operate alone in this.

The subject is vast and it requires **faith, trust** and honest **insight** into oneself and some idea who and what levels may be involved. It is best not to take oneself too seriously. We are only the operator and don't need to know either the sender or the receiver or what is being exchanged on an energy level.

Our job and particularity is **being physical** and thus able to do things

that non-physical beings cannot do. They in turn can do many things that we cannot do. We have complementary roles. Of course, when we begin to care and be interested in the tasks and difficulties of the beings involved this brings respect, love and more understanding into a context where we have clearly come to the limits of our ignorance and irresponsibility concerning nature and our ecosystem.

In a distant harp healing session, I always use a form of prayer then I play harp for about 5-10 minutes. I then check that the request energy line has gone and meditate on what has happened. I choose the mode and starting note completely intuitively and feel my way into the unfoldment of the notes.

harmonic minor
2122131

Distant Healing with the Harp part 2

Part 2 includes a number of practical reflections that I have recorded in a diary form. We'll be looking on how to send distant healing with the harp. My purpose is to encourage other harpists to be open to a wider understanding of the effects of distant healing with their harp. A number of questions come up sooner or later when playing for distant healing as it is somewhat new ground. Obviously, everyone has to find their own way. There is not just one way of doing this. I feel it will be helpful to have more exploration, sharing, and discussion about this theme. I would be interested in hearing your ideas, questions, and experiences - please feel free to write to me.

There are, according to the Harp Distant Healing Think Tank (see page 28), several hundred harpists around the world who have the potential to send distant healing with their harp playing. Most don't realize it. That is why I am writing about this.

It is likely that we have a limited understanding of distant healing in general and distant healing with the harp in particular. Belief and faith are essential and it also helps to understand somewhat how it works. Over the years I have thought a great deal about the methodology of communicating with invisible beings of all kind. It is a tricky subject but we can learn to handle it. I have written about it on my webpage www.vallonperret.com.

1.9.2019 – **Widening circles in the reflector ether**
                 by the minute after distant harp healing
Today I played for 5 minutes on the pedal harp bearing in my heart the theme of distant healing. Immediately afterwards I wanted to sense on Google maps the circle of energy it had created around the harp and house. I had sensed before the effects of concerts. As I understand it, the energy is spreading in the upper part of our etheric energy field called the warmth or reflector ether. After 2 minutes it seemed to have widened to a circle of 100 m distance from the house. The map shows you the continuous expansion, that spread out a bit like ripples in the water. After about 12 minutes I could feel that the circle of energy had

practically covered the whole earth. I was amazed. I cannot determine what it exactly did nor how it could be felt 'out there', but something was happening. Imagine a number of harpists around the world creating daily widening ripples like this.

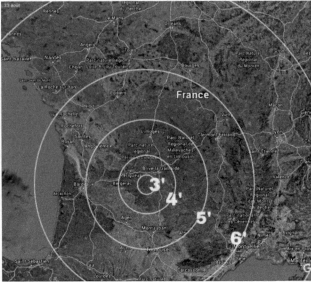

Usually this type of effect ebbs after about 24 hours. Therefore, **daily distant healing** certainly makes sense. We might call this type of distant healing with the harp 'general' as opposite to 'directed distant healing' when directed towards specific areas or beings.

I am used to sensing energy, but it is rare that I sense energy moving on a map. It was with the help of the Hartmann antenna that I could feel how the circle was widening constantly. You need not believe or understand it right away. You can learn to sense and understand energy yourself. I am bringing this forward so it may open our thinking to the possibility of harp playing having a wider effect than we originally might think. We are simply here to serve and contribute to uplifting the energy in difficult times. I will add below the definition of the reflector ether given by Bob Moore, my teacher (see p. 100). Beyond this, I cannot say much, except that the spirit beings tell me that my playing today was drawing on inspiration from sphere 12. Sphere 12 brings the contact to Archai Angels, also known as 'Principalities'; they represent thought, mind and consciousness. (see page 94 or my book on 'Creating Divine Art').

The Harp distant healing think tank
Most of the information in this article comes from what I call the 'Harp distant healing think tank', a group of spirit beings. As I understand it at the moment, it was created in 2019 in response to a request from a Seraphim (sphere 20 angel). Seraphim angels are facilitators behind those harpists who have the potential to send distant healing. See page 8 the drawing illustrating the Seraphim energy field around some harpists. The Harp healing think tank appears to have at the moment six permanent members: Saint Cecilia (the patron of musicians), Emma an 11th century Irish nun who was interested in the effects of musical instruments, a female harpist from Vega (from the constellation of Lyra), Paracelsus, medical doctor (1493-1541), Alice Coltrane (American jazz harpist (1937-2007), Bob Moore, spiritual teacher working with sound (1928-2008).

Anyone contributing to the understanding of distant healing with the harp seems to be automatically connected and is in one way or another contributing to this think tank. In November 2019 there seem to be nearly 700 harpists in the world who potentially have this Seraphim energy around them.

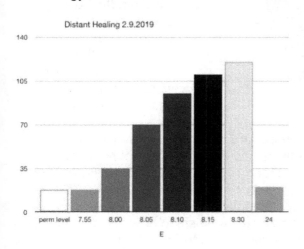

Distant Healing 2.9.2019

3.9.19 - **Distant healing**
The type of energy at work in distant healing is simply universal love. It comes from the level of Throne angels, then moves into the reflector ether (also called warmth ether) where it stays available for a while for the person to let it sink in, according to their openness and willingness to change. Each person or being is operating at a

certain energy level at a specific time. Each period of distant healing brings some additional energy to the person (or being) that they may be able to integrate to various degrees as time goes by. In the two tables below, we see measurements of the energy level of this group of healers at 7.55 a.m. up to 8.30 and 24 h later. The distant healing time of that group lasts from 8-8.15 a.m. The values on the left scale are mainly means to compare and don't mean much in absolute (here somewhat arbitrary) values.

A is a normally healthy person. E is a person with breast cancer undergoing life prolonging treatment. The permanent energy level (white bar on left) refers to their general energy level on the physical plane (etheric, mental, etc.) whereas the various blue bars refer to the love energy coming in. White and blue bars are thus not directly comparable.

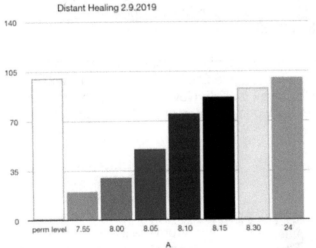

Distant Healing 2.9.2019

Although a person may not be able to fully integrate the healing energy on the physical plane, she would usually benefit from the love energy on her soul level, which is not possible to show in this graph.

Distant healing with the harp and other music instruments

Mid-September 2019 I noticed new energy fields around practically all the instruments in my music room. They are the by now 'known fields' discovered around the harp earlier on that year: the spiritual field and the five elements and their elementals. That makes 6 concentric fields around any instrument. The Seraphim seem to have initiated them. I am told that now all these instruments in the room can actively contribute to a healing process on the level of the five elements and their elementals (on the smallest levels these elementals are the gnomes, undines, salamander, sylphs, and the 5th type elementals). This includes effects on the etheric of humans, animals, and plants – present or at distance. Any musician has the potential to do this and acquire these six fields around their musical instruments.

The conditions for a musician are: a non-egotistic motivation (that implies having transformed the energy of the three lower chakras), an open heart and well-functioning thyroid chakra, as well as being familiar with prayer and distant healing. Prayer implies being open to the divine field, distant healing requires trust and faith in one's own capacities (of cooperation with the invisible).

The harp remains an instrument with an additional and unique potential, being able to be used for all types of present and distant healing, including animals and human beings. We are talking here mainly about distant healing; any instrument can of course transmit beautiful music and uplift. This specific potential of the harp again is nothing to get a big head about, as 'big head' means big ego and instantly destroys an individual's capacity to take part in this type of healing, whether with a harp or with other instruments.

This practice or knowledge of using musical instruments to help the elementals and nature was according to the 'harp distant think tank', known in 16th century Sussex by people in connection with contemporary Swiss Alchemist and medical Doctor Paracelsus. Before this it possibly was known by the Celts on the continent and in Ancient Egypt. It shows though that this practice was used but it was rare, maybe because of a number of conditions having to come together to make it work, as those mentioned above.

The transformation of the three lower chakras, the opening of the heart, the genuine opening to prayer and finding the trust in distant healing are not easily achieved. We may for instance not have thought much about prayer and be used to a mechanical ritual way of praying, yet quite closed off to the Divine for instance. It helps to get clear within

ourselves about the concept of God or a Creator.
And that is only one of possible challenges.

22.9.2019 - Today, during my workshop on
Spiritual Healing, I used the Egyptian Bow harp
that I had built by a local harp maker. I tuned it to
the **Aulos/Schlesinger tonal system** which was
probably used in Ancient Egypt; it is best played in
a non-melodic way without chords. The eight
energy fields quite quickly built up around both the
harp and the crystal (see in front of harp on the
carpet); the lines of the Deva and the Landscape
angel that had converged towards the crystal both
disappeared while playing for them as the course
participants could sense as well. I then played for
another five minutes for global (undirected) distant
healing and immediately afterwards we could all
observe how the circle widened on Google maps.

Using the Aulos undertone scales shows it does actually not matter
what tonal system or mode you play in, but what is important is how
and with what kind of intention you play. All the while the 315° 'Think
Tank' segment around the crystal remained perceivable. This is
certainly a sign from the 'Harp healing think tank' to keep working on
the subject.

18.11.2019 - **a particular way of playing**
Distant healing with the harp needs a particular way of playing that
pulls away completely from being concerned with how our play might
impress others. The technicality of our play becomes irrelevant and
gets in the way. It is not about 'how does the listener like what I do',
otherwise an element of fear comes in and disturbs the process. Fast
and acrobatic playing are irrelevant, even melodies. All that seems to
'matter' is the depth our feeling or heart contact. Then harp playing
becomes a prayer. The ego steps aside as it is not allowed to
participate. The very much unused parts of the third eye or pineal

chakra take over (see page 107). I have published a booklet on the chakras and how to access the hidden potential of the pineal. Published only in French and German at the moment. If enough requests, I can translate it into English.

Practicing this kind of harp playing is not difficult. We just need to drop restrictive concepts and play only what feels right in the moment. For instance, silence and space between notes are often unconscious taboos in our music. So, it is all about the interpretation, the how and not about what we play. No dogmas needed. If e.g. you feel better with A = 432 Hz, do it.

20.11.19 - The Soul contact in distant healing

See-feeling the energy structure around the quartz crystal belonging to the contact with the distant harp healing thinktank is spurring me on to explore more about distant healing with our harps.

The contact with our own soul 'matters'. But what is the soul? Many people talk about it meaning a deep contact with themselves. That is of course true. But then, what is a genuine deep contact with ourselves? This matters in sound healing in general, but even more so in distant healing with the harp, as the transfer happens on a deep level of energy, we know very little about. 'Energy' meaning invisible, barely understood levels of consciousness.

When looking at our own energy fields, moving out from our physical body, we first contact the etheric, then the lower astral level, which is the home for painful emotions (sorrow, anger, frustrations, jealousy, feelings of inferiority/superiority, fear, insecurity, etc.). Moving out a little further, we come in contact with feelings, which are transformed painful emotions and belong to the upper astral energy field. They become compassion, serenity, joy, generosity, being at peace, etc. This brings us to the spiritual or quality part of our own aura. We may think that this is the end of feelings, yet, beyond this we get into what we could call refined, spiritual, or higher feelings. These have nothing to do with the feeling of the upper astral. Beyond our quality aura (see drawing page 103) we enter the vast field of our timeless soul and what we might loosely call the divine field. In that space we do not have any other means of observation than our higher or subtle feelings, as more often than not, we don't get any pictures or anything recognizable. We just may distinguish different feeling qualities.

In order to get a real and deeper feeling contact with our soul, we need to accept, that there is a life between the physical lives on earth. That is the space we come from before birth and go back to after death. That is where the timeless part of our soul resides. It is the mind stream that exists over many, often hundreds of our earthly lives. In order to have a deep soul contact with ourselves, we don't necessarily need to have a contact to past lives. We though need an ever-deepening feeling contact with what we can call our life or soul purpose for this incarnation.

What we can call our 'soul path' is a narrow path following the call or tasks defined by our soul before conception. Our spiritual aura contains our spiritual ray colors. There are seven rays (see page 45). We may have, in this life, one or two of them there, visible for clairvoyants. Lately I seem to get an understanding that these colors are related to our resonant tone(s).

Why does a deep soul contact matter for distant harp healing? Once we have accepted the existence of past lives, quality colors and the existence of a soul path, or tasks we have agreed on to try to fulfill in this life, we very likely would be open to our deeper, soul level feelings, that give us the direction to follow. We may once in a while get a subtle hint. Other times we may have to be reminded through suffering what our contract, or deeper feelings are.

I remember cutting into one of my fingers with a chain saw. For a harpist it is as close as you can get to disaster. Luckily all healed well with practically no sequel. Yet, it made me realize that I had neglected a deeper feeling dimension in leaving a team of a spiritual healing center. Once I had contacted it, shed a few genuine tears, I realized how deep my commitment and link had been, even if it was meant to be only temporarily. The deep feeling contact came back fully into my awareness and I stayed on linking to the energy of that geographically distant place. I continue since then to be part of their distant healing group of healers.

28.11.2019 - How to target distant harp healing?

As mentioned above the importance in distant harp healing is a deep feeling connection. An abstract, good intention type of connection alone does not work, as I discovered in the following example. I saw a report on the television about the abominable conditions of refugees on the eastern Greek islands these days of late 2019 and this prompted me to include them in my next distant healing. However, for some reason that remained too abstract and general for me to connect to today. Yet, when I thought about the massive number of Koala bears that died in the bush fires of 2019, as they were unable to escape, my heart immediately responded. Koala bears are now a species threatened with extinction, also because their natural food resources have burnt.

I started to play for them. A very unexpected way of playing imposed itself, playing in simple octaves in the very low range, non-melodic, moving at times along half tone steps. My deep feelings remained with the playing, opening a flow of intensity, light, and even joy, ending in a more usual flow of notes in the upper range. I knew this type of octave playing from the aulos scales on the Egyptian bow harp. Every note (octave interval) requires full presence and intensity.

29.11.2019 – Four types of Harp Distant Healing

I have observed four types:

1) Requests coming from **a specific nature spirit or landscape angel**, through the intermediary of the quartz crystal. A line is showing up at the crystal, indicating the contact, the geographic direction and, on request also the distance and the type of request, including the explicit wish for me playing the harp. Here I play usually for 5 minutes, after which the line disappears and the being confirms the action has worked.

2) No particular request noticed. I play for 10 minutes **for nature and its nature spirits in general**. I can sense in Google maps the widening circle in the warmth (reflector) ether that eventually spreads over the whole planet.

3) Request coming from **a person**. I need a photograph, name of the person and the request either by mail or visual contact. I play for 10 minutes and ask the person, if possible, to sit during the same time and be open to receive. During this time, I build up a feeling contact to the person.

4) I often play **for a group** of animals or beings in need. No explicit request has been formulated. I play for five to ten minutes. I usually receive some kind of response afterwards with the help of my Hartmann antenna, from a group soul of those animals, another spirit being and/or from the think tank contact. In all of this it is very important to build up your own feeling/heart contact.

2.12.19 – perceiving the effects of Distant Harp Healing

It is one thing to get oneself in the right frame of mind for sending distant healing. But what can we suggest to the person receiving it? This will mostly depend on how aware and open the person is. It is best to agree on a time, 10 minutes is sufficient; it is not the length of time that will make the difference. The best you can transfer will happen within these 10 minutes. If you come to a different conclusion, just make sure what your motivation is and try out different lengths of time.

It is best when we have talked to the person before sending healing so we can connect in a feeling way. Do not focus on problems but rather reach a depth of contact within ourselves - that is with the divine dimension. The person can sit or lie down and simply be aware of feelings on the different levels: body sensations, emotions, feelings, thoughts, memories, intuitions, involuntary pictures, etc. Ideally, we should have an exchange afterwards at some point, either verbal or written as we may be able to help the person to be aware of important aspects she has observed.

As an example: even falling briefly asleep can be very useful and significant, as this is a time when the usual intellectual control gives way to something else happening. The effects may last up to 36 hours after the distant healing, in dreams e.g. or other symptoms, as in a different thought patterns appearing. It is not necessarily so different from receiving distant healing without a harp, as similar non-physical beings and energies may be involved. Yet, as I have described earlier on, the harp IS a special instrument and involves different beings. It may require from the harpist some training to be able to assist the person in this process. All spiritual healing is also a process of spiritual growth for the healer.

7.12.19 - the aim of healing

At my talk yesterday evening some of these energy lines and beings showed up around the quartz crystal and requested distant harp healing. I played 5 minutes with that intention and all the lines disappeared. Playing this time on the Ancient Egyptian bow harp with its special **Schlesinger scale**, I played simply in octaves. It was improvised as this scale does not lend itself to melodies or chords. I personally find that avoiding melodies helps me just to concentrate on the flow and not be focused on playing it right or on memorizing.

Distant harp healing is about intention, feeling, flow, best with no hindrances interfering. Ultimately **the aim of healing** is not physical health, although this may improve as well, but being in peace with ourselves, with our life's purpose, our alignment with our timeless soul.

8.12.19 - Invisible beings assist us

When we play harp as a kind of prayer with the intention of sending healing, we are never alone in this. Invisible beings assist us, mostly beings from the angelic realm. We contribute what we are best at, they do the same. We let ourselves go into the river of energy, the feeling, the intensity, the flow. It is crucial to learn to trust the river, which is the energy of the divine field including the energy of the Black Virgin, the Mother Earth Goddess, the creative womb. We must leave our 'clothes' (our ego and persona) on the river bank.

15.12.19 - Levels of harp distant healing

I observe with different harpists differences in the energy fields around their harps. This is due to different degrees of distant healing, as I understand it. My dialogue with the 'Harp distant healing think tank' has brought following explanations. When a harp is built, the Archangel Raphael, patron of harps and healing, attributes one of his angels to the instrument. One can easily sense it as an energy column standing next to the harp, often to one side of it.

When a harpist starts to dedicate some of their playing to healing, another quality comes into their playing. This is the case for any harp therapist, I presume, as well as harpists who play for distant healing. The five concentric energy fields related to the five elements and their elementals establish themselves around the harp as well as the spiritual field. For this to happen the harpist needs to develop a non-egotistic attitude and a kind of praying mood whilst playing. This energy connection brings the faculty of playing for nature, trees, areas, rivers, nature spirits and potentially for elementals of all sizes. These elementals go from very small ones (gnomes, undines, salamander, sylphs, no 5 elementals, fairies, devas, and suchlike) up to possibly very large elementals like spirits of river systems, mountains, etc. I understand that we are gradually given access to these different levels. It is needless to say that these processes only work through the intermediary of light beings of the spiritual world.

When a harpist reaches further levels of purity, devotion, compassion, and selflessness other fields are added. There is the energy field of the Sepharim angels. I sense it several meters away from the harp. From then on distant healing can be sent efficiently to humans or animals (individuals or group souls of animals). A mental field brings the capacity to direct energy intentionally. At some later stage the capacity to send distant healing to insects is added. This is not yet the final stage as there probably will always remain wider possibilities to be accessed.

1.1.2020
May 2020 and the near future bring us more understanding about the (distant) healing potential of the harp. Playing for Australia today made me realize even more how distant healing needs the consent of those we play for. In tuning into the recent fires in Australia I realized that a

large fire elemental was at work and did not wish me to interfere at that moment. (I have a number of years of experience connecting to large elementals.) I then reduced my focus and played for the Australian squirrels because I could more easily relate to them with my feelings. A larger focus (landscape, humans, forest areas) was for me not possible at that moment to connect in a feeling way.

4.1.2020 - **Harp distant healing for people** is a little different. Everyone needs to find their own way to go about it. Five to ten minutes playing is fine. We need to realize that once we feel that we are able to contribute to this level of playing, that we are assisted by light beings. These beings provide the particular type of healing energy.

An essential step, beyond our own preparations, is to help the receiver(s) to open themselves to that energy. A preliminary talk together to build a basis for trust and understanding is necessary. I am not necessarily talking about a therapeutic intervention, but at least a human caring contact. Anything from one to a number of talks may be helpful. We can play for a number of people at the same time as it is not so much about healing a particular problem but about assisting a flow of divine energy to circulate.

We also need to get clear about a number of issues here : what is spiritual healing, what and who is being healed, what are the energies involved, who is doing the healing, what can we contribute to help the person be receptive, what type of playing is best, how can we know that we are on the required level of playing, how and how long after can any results be observed, how can we deepen our feeling contact with it all?

Obviously, there is a limit to what a written text like this can contribute to finding real answers to these questions. Courses can be an opportunity to explore this together.

11.1.2020 - **On the nature of distant healing**

While hands on healing, or any form of healing that takes place while the person is present, can operate on different levels directly: physical, etherically, astrally, mentally and spiritually, distant healing mainly works on the spiritual level plus the reflector ether and the upper mental level. It is the contact with the spiritual level that allows a person to re-align themselves with their timeless soul and the divine field. In so doing a process of becoming aware of life hindering beliefs takes place, allowing a gradual dissolution of these beliefs; the energy of love and truth can replace them. This process is enhanced with the conscious co-operation of the receiver and it is only when the unconscious contrary belief structures are reached that transformation can happen.

Otherwise only a temporary relief can take place and sooner or later the unconscious patterns will take over again and affect e.g. the physical, mental, and emotional health. Our deep beliefs rule our life and bring us everything we meet. In a similar way, the limitations of the healer can diminish the purity of the love energy they send in distant healing. These possible limitations on both sides will determine the observable results of distant healing (with or without harp). Changing and transforming beliefs is the key to moving on, moving closer to the intelligence of the universe, the divine unified field. Basically, it comes down to choosing and working with tools, methods and practices that prove truly transformative for ourselves. Real transformation can be observed as concrete, lasting changes happening in our daily life.

Distant healing directed to nature spirits and elementals is often easier, as they are without ego problems that may hinder the working of distant healing. Nature spirits and elementals do not have a mind. They have a consciousness which is not the same as having a mind.

29.3.2020 – **The importance of emptying oneself**

The think tank asks me to stress the importance of emptying oneself of any concepts, being natural and playful as an attitude in distant healing.

15.4.2020 – Prayer, Distant Healing with and without harp
What is the difference? DH with harp builds upon the depth of feeling and the overtone space between two notes. This combination produces the best DH results. The energy traveling in the upper reflector ether creates the 'widening ring in the water' effect as seen in the map page 28. Depth of feeling is enhanced when the harpist raises their vibration to ultimately attract a Seraphim energy field around them combined with a mind field (of essentially upper mental energy). A prayerful attitude may be added, which would again enhance the effects. When all these aspects come together there is fundamentally no difference from one harpist to another. The overtones of the harp played in the described manner are the closest we can come to the music of the spheres. That is the particular contribution in distant healing with a harp or a similar instrument, enabling thus the highest energy contact we can achieve. This of course includes a co-operation with beings of the divine field.

In DH without the harp there is also in a transmission of healing energy through the upper reflector ether. The quality or depth achieved depends on the contact the healer has reached within themselves and on the openness of the receiver.

During prayer a contact from heart to heart is established, meaning a spiritual contact from the divine in us to the divine in the other person.

23.4.20
We may at times experience the despair, the suffering, and the immense uncertainty that so many are feeling during the present period. It is important to accept this. It helps to include these painful feelings when we play the harp, even for only five minutes. We can at the same time bring in our thoughts for distant healing and then return to our daily activity. Our distant healing playing will be deeper if we bring ourselves in with all that we are truly feeling at the time. We don't always need to be in a 'perfectly' balanced mood. I am not talking about a cathartic therapy session for ourselves but just about starting from where we are at there and then.

Getting more depth into our improvisation

It is basically very simple …yet quite demanding as it takes us on a journey that gives us access to nothing less than the divine dimension of sound and energy as well as the depth in us.

Simple, because it is about using our feelings and not about playing techniques, intellectual concepts and reading notes. It is just about feelings. Just two notes can be played with great depth of feeling.
It is also demanding because we often have a complicated relationship to our feelings. Let me use a quote from my teacher Bob Moore, about feelings:

"It's very difficult to produce descriptions of feeling. Having worked with people for many years now, it seems to me that the word feeling has been strongly related to emotion. One can look at feeling and find that if one follows the movement through emotional conditions within us, one of course is drawn to feeling. One can look at that and say that it is the upper bracket of emotion*. It is. But then that doesn't end the connection to feeling. In fact, one can say that is only the beginning.** "
* Bob is talking about the feelings of the upper astral: serenity, calmness, joy, compassion, etc.
** Those higher feelings cannot be described easily with words. Often, we need metaphors to describe the differences observed on that level.

This accurately describes the journey towards a deeper connection with the divine field. What are the steps made of?

This distinction between different types of feelings is very important for getting the necessary depth in our harp playing in distant healing. Playing pleasant melodies or improvising on musical modes is fine and often the best thing one should do when playing in a hospital room because they lead you into upper astral feelings. However, a good harpist will go beyond that when playing modes and melodies and they will access another layer. I experience this as if the floor becomes transparent underneath the feet and opens up to another dimension 'below' it. 'Below' is not exact as it opens into another dimension all together. The exploration of the feeling in the five elements can lead you directly into going beyond the upper astral into higher feelings.

I describe further on in the chapter about playing the space underneath the surface of a lake for instance. If you have gone beyond the fear of deep water in yourself, you can enjoy the silence, the space, the slowness of that space. It connects you to a very deep feeling close to the energy of the Black Virgin or the night sky. And this is clearly beyond the upper astral feelings. My discovery of the link between the five elements, music and the human energy field came while studying the subtle anatomy with Bob Moore. It is only now that I realise that the five elements create a direct bridge into spaces beyond the astral, a depth that brings the energy of the spiritual level into our playing.

I don't think there are general rules fitting everyone. It is a personal journey. Our musical education has unfortunately often followed in the footsteps of the general intellectual approach in our culture. Note reading, learning all kinds of information about a composer's life, music theory, underlining brilliance in performance, competition, impressing others are some of the obstacles to impede us from connecting with our feelings in music. Having gone through a conventional musical education, many people cannot even imagine improvising.

Once Improvisation is free of idioms, they are essentially based on following our feelings. We can also improvise by playing a melody of course, as long as the feeling contact is not lost through too much concentration on technique and on not making errors. For distant healing with the harp to work effectively, we just need to deepen our feeling contact with what we are doing.

Joel Goldsmith, in his wonderful book of 'Spiritual Healing', advises that healers stop thinking about a person's problem and concentrate on our contact to the divine within us. We need to drop all preconceived ideas and play from our heart (and not our head). The rest is taken care of by spirit beings and the laws of energy.

We must keep in mind: in distant healing with the harp, the receiver is not physically present and therefore cannot hear and see what we play. What is transmitted is energy, it is only felt and works much like a prayer. The only difference is that we have the magical help of the harp, its' overtones and the spirit beings connected with it.

Some doors into improvisation

When I started playing the harp, I felt I needed total freedom in playing it and only free improvisation could do that for me. The following approaches have been very useful on my path.

The sound of the harp is my first guide into feeling the music. I especially enjoy the very low notes and love recording them with a microphone very close to the harp.

Indian music approach: Listen to classical Indian music and especially the Dhrupad style and Alap part of ragas. This can teach you how to get into the depth of a single note, a single interval, how to approach that note in a timeless way.

From Indian raga music I learned to **play over a drone**, a single note or a constant chord and enjoy the various tensions produced by each interval. The think tank tells me to emphasize the conscious feeling use of intervals, as they are the doors of inspiration. No interval is wrong, they have different atmospheres and tensions, thus asking for more or less space to follow.

Two chord trance: While I avoid being stuck in a repetitive series of the same 3-4 chords, using alternating two chords can bring you into trance like music.

I have explored and **use unusual modes and scales** extensively, as they lead me away from being stuck in a repetitive melody.

Very common in improvisation is to **use a tune or a fragment of a tune at the beginning and at the end** of an improvisation. From there you launch into a thorough exploration of the intervals used or the musical ideas in it.

Using **imagery from the five elements** has been immensely beneficial for me. Avoid mimicking the element too much. What helps is to explore the feeling of it. For instance, playing the feeling of the space of water beneath the surface, the buzzard flying high above in the sunny sky, etc. Each element can lead us into an endless variety of its different aspects as for instance with water: rain, fog, storm, cascade, surface of a lake, waves, gurgling brook.

Correspondences between the 7 spiritual rays and the fundamental 'spiritual' note of a person
probably most accurate on the basis of 432 Hz

I received this is information from C, as far as the notes are concerned. The color-quality connection has been known for a long time. It was taught by Bob Moore. I personally do not have enough tested examples with spiritual notes of a person. Please feel free to explore and test it. The persons I have tested it with, responded very well.

		1	2	3
red	courage, will power, independence, leadership	C	– C⁺	- D
orange	balance, harmony, rhythm, beauty	D	– D⁺	- E
yellow	tolerance, patience, logic, precision	E	– F	– F⁺
green	impartiality, adaptability, instinctual power, mental power	F	– F⁺	– G
blue	intuition, love, wisdom, perception	G	– G⁺	– A
rose pink	devotion, loyalty, service to others, directness	A	– A⁺	– B
violet	truth, rituals, action, integrity, vitality, dignity	B	– C	– C⁺

The spiritual rays are found in our spiritual aura, about 1 meter away from our physical body. This layer is also called the quality aura. Everybody has mainly one or two colors. There is no hierarchy in these colors. They are a set of spiritual qualities every soul has got to assimilate over many life times. Usually a soul stays several life times on a ray. When a person has her first life on a ray, she would most likely feel a level **1** note is her note. In successive lives on a same ray she will tend to move up to **2** and level **3**. People with two rays in their spiritual aura, will likely resonate with two fundamental notes. The more developed rays possibly react stronger.

The 7 favorable modes: Ionian, Dorian, Lydian, Mixolydian, Eolian, melodic Minor, harmonic minor

A second type of resonating note can sometimes be found; it is of a more astral/emotional kind. A person less in contact with their spiritual qualities would react to a note related to a particularly well transformed chakra, where they have developed a strength. Heart chakra F > compassion; solar plexus E > love & understanding, etc. That note can vary one note up or down, depending on how much that chakra is developed. The more developed the higher the particular note.

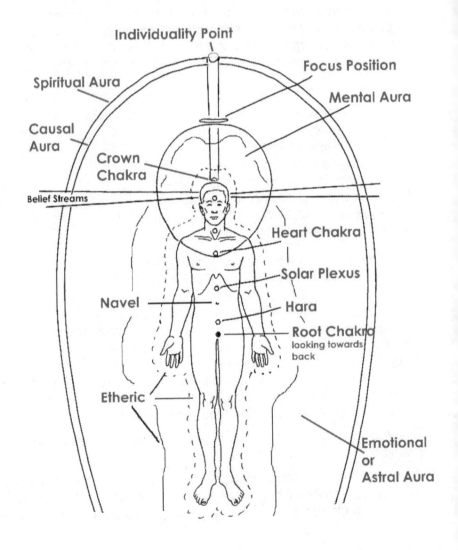

The 5 Elements in Music

The feeling Quality in an interpretation

How does one appreciate and distinguish the feeling quality of a piece of music? The same piece played by two different harpists will have a different feeling and a different quality. How does that come about and how can we improve the subtle quality of our playing, as this determines the quality of what is sent in distant healing?

The metaphor of the 5 elements is a unique way of relating sound, feeling and the inner aspects of our energy system. Our western five elements have been embedded in our culture for centuries: astrological birth charts, the elemental types of nature spirits, our metaphors, etc. This makes it natural for us to feel what the qualities of *earth, water, fire, air* and *space* are. We can easily hear and feel them when someone plays, dances, sings. In groups people are astonished how easy and natural it is to pick up the quality of what a person plays. It is best perceived when we play in an improvised non-melodic, sound scape type of way. When we are too attached to melodies, modes, playing chords, and rhythms it can be helpful to take an instrument or use a mode we cannot reproduce these aspects with. Then we can concentrate on the feeling quality of what we are trying to express. A frame drum, flower pots, a mode totally unfamiliar to us can help us access the simplicity of our feelings. This is easier than we think and is playful and very enjoyable. Maybe the difficult bit, for some, is to combine imagining a particular state of an element and get into the feeling of it. Take the example of a little brook. You don't just want to mimic the acoustic part of its gurgling waters. You need to imagine a leaf or a little paper boat floating and bobbing up and down on the water. Then you get the feeling of the aliveness of the water movement. Another example is to get the feeling of water beneath the surface of a pond, lake or sea. (The awareness of the five elements was important for the 16th century medical doctor Paracelsus, a member of the think tank for harp distant healing.)

A qualitative observation

Numerous phenomena – especially musical ones – remain incomprehensible to the intellect, if one responds to them only with the left side of the brain. It is these phenomena that have always attracted me. I have therefore endeavoured to find ways to observe, discern and understand them better. I have listened to a great deal of non-melodic music that one may call '**soundscapes**' or 'sound paintings'. They may particularly suit a qualitative approach. The more I listen, the more I can perceive ways to discern differences in quality. What is such discernment actually responding to, since there is often no melody, no tonality and no rhythm in these soundscapes? In my training programme I let people listen, for instance, to recordings of six different didgeridoo players and six different musicians playing on singing bowls. Why do we perceive differences of quality with singing bowls ? A bowl is struck from time to time, yet within seconds we get a clear impression emanating from the way they are played. This is not due to the quality of the bowls themselves, but rather to the way they are played.

On recordings of didgeridoos you can more or less hear just one note. The playing technique is roughly the same and not necessarily very varied. Yet again we may experience a clear sense of a distinct quality pouring out of every recording. The different qualities experienced cannot be explained logically. The first time I became puzzled by this phenomenon was when looking for a suitable version of the 'Gavotte en Rondo' taken from the partitas for solo violin by J.S. Bach. I went to a public library that luckily had five or six different versions of that Gavotte. While comparing them I realised how different the versions of this same musical score were. I finally chose a version played by Itzhak Perlman, which I perceived to be the only one showing a very good balance between the male and female sides. Generally speaking, our left side of the body is our receptive, feminine side, our link to emotions and feelings, to where we are at. It relates to the right hemisphere of our brain. The right side refers to expression, the male aspect, the step we take towards something and is linked to the left hemisphere of the brain. How should I try to understand the difference of quality in all the versions I listened to ?

The same question arose when I listened to six different female singers interpreting songs by Saint Hildegard of Bingen. From the first seconds of each interpretation I was aware of distinct differences in quality. I could on many occasions verify with friends and course participants, musicians and non-musicians alike, that the perception of these differences was largely a common experience.

The first album of meditative music I ever composed was in 1981. I played on a superb Steinway grand piano and tried to catch the atmospheres of seven different trees. It is impossible to describe logically how to render the particular energy of a tree merely though music. I remember playing those recordings to a class of primary school children and asking them to draw what they heard and felt. They did not know which music represented which tree, yet they were able easily to detect which one was the birch and which one the oak. They were equally able to express their impressions using coloured pencils on paper.

In my courses I suggest that participants represent their impressions of one of their colleagues by improvising a soundscape type of music. I give them mostly non-melodic instruments to work with because they encourage the creation of sound paintings: a drum, flower pots, an African balafon not tuned to our piano notes, etc. I often give someone a specific task such as playing 'a mountain' or 'a large slow-moving river', a task that can seem insurmountable at first. It is very interesting to discover how well most people are able to create in their playing the exact atmosphere of the subject given to them and that the listeners can actually pick up the very same image that I had whispered into the musician's ear before starting the exercise.

Using **metaphors, images and symbols**, allows us to express dimensions that are largely unknown to the intellect. With their help we can grasp the mysterious, the magic at work. Although we sometimes believe we can catch the essence of a phenomenon with the help of words, we often realise later on that this is largely an illusion. However, there are certain words that can reveal a number of unexpected layers of understanding. This is well known in healing, cultural and religious traditions that have been using the system of the five elements for centuries if not millennia. Those who developed these systems knew that engaging with the five elements in a metaphorical way would somehow help them to express their glimpses of the mysterious. They also knew that anything they could say about any one of the elements, its correspondences on the physical and non-physical levels would be only 'finger pointing' in the right direction. The five-element system would never serve to touch or represent the phenomenon itself. Accordingly, the use of symbols and metaphors may serve to bring us closer to the truth than we would get if we responded on a purely intellectual level.

In order to discern the quality of what is being played it is essential to listen and respond with the help of the right hemisphere of the brain, thus using feelings, intuition and overall impressions. After doing this we can bring into play the brain's left hemisphere to analyse what we have just heard with some precision. How do the right brain processes work ?

Millenary old traditions

So as to understand and express laws operating in the natural world, mankind has evolved numerous models. One of these is the Chinese yin and yang system that lead to the development of a system named the five phases of energy, sometimes mistakenly called the five 'elements' system, a corner stone of traditional Chinese medicine. I use the five elements system as known in Ancient Greece, in India and in Tibet. Since 1980, I have been developing this approach in my work as a music therapist with a great variety of people including people with special needs, prisoners, children and adults who come to my training programmes in different countries. I also use this approach in my work as a musician, as a music teacher and as a composer. As one of my principal sources of inspiration I would like to name Bob Moore. I have enjoyed books from the anthroposophical tradition as well as from Indian, Chinese and Tibetan traditions (Bertelsen, J. 1982; Diolosa, C.,

2000; Gamborg, H. 1998; Irwin, E., 1988; Khenchen Thrangu, 2002; Peukert, W.-E., 1976; Saraswati, S. 2000; Satyangananda, S., 2000; Wangyal, T., 2002).

The ideal state of an element is its balance relative to the other four elements together with its own evolution towards a more spiritual level. Each element is then in a continuous dynamic of evolutionary change and is in an unending search for balance due to the constantly changing world in which it appears. We can easily observe the characteristics of a metaphorical element by noting how that element appears in nature. We refer to all the five elements together as a metaphor in order to understand better how they may function on an inner level. Each element exists within us in its emotional aspect. It can though be transformed into its feeling or spiritual counterpart.

The element *earth* for instance is strongly associated with any sense of 'insecurity' and its counterpart **security** and self-acceptance. The *water* element is connected to anger which is opposed by **calmness** as well as by vitality and physical well-being. *Fire* is associated with fear and its counterpart the qualities of **love** and understanding. The *air* element may be used to discern either **joy** or depression and self-pity and *space* element may reveal either suppression or its opposite the qualities of **expression** and silence.

In Tibetan medicine the same five elements are traditionally linked to the first five energy centres or chakras and to an ideal state of being that personal evolution aspires to attain (Khenhen Thrangu, 2002). 'Chakra' is the name used in Hinduism for an energy centre (see chapter one). The five-element metaphor gives an access to practices of inner transformation in the different Tibetan traditions, Buddhist, Bön, Dzogchen and tantra as well as in the Indian traditions, yoga, Buddhist and tantra). The roots of these traditions go back several millennia and they offer a very detailed understanding of the five elements and how they form our world.

The five elements system provides a fundamental metaphor that helps us to understand the dynamic that underlies different modern scientific disciplines such as chemistry, physics, medicine and psychology.

Tenzin Wangyal Rinpoche writes: "Through an understanding of the elements we can see that apparently different dimensions of experience are really only subtler and grosser levels of the elements. An excess of fire, for example, manifests in physical, energetic, mental and spiritual dimensions…. So, fire is the life-giving energy of the sun as well as the life-destroying forest fire." For Tenzin Wangyal fire is " the heat of the digestive system, the creativity of the mind, the red light of the rainbow, the phenomenon of temperature, the emotions of hatred and desire, the warmth of compassion, the wisdom of discrimination, and one of the five most subtle and most fundamental aspects of being." (Tenzin Wangyal Rinpoche, 2002)

The five-element metaphor allows us to understand a number of phenomena. It allows us to glimpse the laws at work that gave us five fingers, five toes, five major senses, five major categories of emotions and their transformation into five positive aspects, among other things. In the Tibetan approach, again according to Tenzin Wangyal (2002), we can find a healing level that creates a bridge to the traditional Chinese medicine and its five major organs system : *earth*/spleen, *water*/kidneys, *fire*/liver, *air*/lungs, *space*/heart. These pairings link us to the psychosomatic dimension of each major organ which is so well described in Chinese medicine and one of its branches the science of acupuncture meridians.

Tenzin Wangyal Rinpoche also reminds us how each element may bring us pleasure and wellbeing. When we lose ourselves in the vastness of the blue sky or the starry night, it is the element of *space* that nourishes and regenerates us. The flight of the swallows or the hang glider, the movement of the flags in the wind, the full sails of a large sailing ship, the clouds, they all fill us with the generosity of the wind and the element *air*. The flames of a camp *fire* and the light of a candle bring warmth and comfort. A walk on the edge of the *water*, the presence of a cascade, the rain on a summer's day, taking a shower or a bath, pacifies and purifies us. Seeing a mountain or a freshly ploughed field touches us deep within.

In my work as a music therapist I find myself continuously confronted with the perennial question : Is my way of working effective? How can I grasp more accurately the quality of an individual's musical expression, the essence of his difficulties and, of course, the progress made in therapy ? I feel this sense of urgency even more with young children, always aware that it will be much more difficult for them to catch up later on with 'normal' evolution as a result of the time lost because of behavioural patterns which were not remedied before the age of seven or eight.

The primary goals during the music therapy sessions are simple though. I believe it is essential to watch for any sign of **intensity** and **joy** in someone's musical expression. I have the impression that these two qualities work like keys that open doors and make anything possible. How are they connected to someone's development process? What obstructs someone from leading his or her life with intensity and joy ? When I speak of joy, I speak of a direct contact with something in ourselves much deeper than our mundane concerns. Perhaps we make contact with what one calls the soul, a spiritual aspect in us. Detectable intensity seems to bear witness to the total involvement of an individual's essence with his action in the present moment. As soon as joy and intensity are present it would seem that the five resistances to personal evolution and to the discovery of new aspects in us, as taught in Buddhism, vanish : laziness, doubt, sleepiness, anger and restlessness.

Over the years I have come to appreciate the impressive usefulness of the five-element system for the qualitative evaluation of musical expression. The elements metaphor allows us to discover the natural bridges that exist between music and the human being, between interior and exterior. It helps us to understand concretely how much musical expression is a "fingerprint" of the musician, how much his music reflects his whole being. We can learn to detect connections between someone's musical expression and his thought structures, emotions, body areas (with energy blockages), between the subconscious and spirituality, between left and right brain appreciation which is to say between intellect and feeling or intuition. The five elements metaphor allows us to draw a map that connects the quality present in a person's expression, musical or non-musical with his psycho-energetic structure. This allows us better to understand the inner dimension, residing deep within every being. The works by the neurobiologist Colwyn Trevarthen on musicality, the brain and communication confirm this. I return to this further on.

The five elements tool works in two ways : we can use it as a starting point to help a person find a better balance between the elements within and in so doing the different levels, physical, emotional, mental and spiritual will be affected. My hypothesis suggests that a better harmonisation within a person brings about a better musicality, that is an improvement in the quality of her musical expression.

Not only can we see if someone has got *fire* or lacks *earth* or *space* in her musical expression, we can also tell if she is *warm hearted,* has her feet on the *ground,* is *fluid* in her movements and her whole being. "The way we talk, the colours we like, and the way we walk or move our hands, are but expressions of the elements. We can tell, if we know what we are looking for, which element or elements are dominant in us." (Wangyal, 2002)

Qualitative listening assisted by the five elements can also be helpful when working with couples, families or groups. Listening to people playing together will tell us whether they have a tendency to avoid one or more elements in their functioning. As this is about feeling an individual's or group's psycho-energetic aspect, observation with the help of the five elements does not have to be limited to playing a musical instrument. It works just as well with singing, movement, dance, talking and communication in general.

The four elements *earth, water, fire* and *air* have been known in Europe at least since the days of Ancient Greece. They are part of our culture. Many expressions in our everyday language refer to them. We meet the same first four elements in our horoscopes, where each one is associated with three signs of the zodiac. The number of planets you have in any element can give you an indication about the excess or lack of a particular element in your makeup. The traditional system using the four elements was taken up again by Paracelsus in the Middle Ages (a Swiss doctor, 1493-1541). He added to them the fifth element *space* or *ether*.

The need to feel connected to All-There-Is is a human characteristic. It is not, therefore, surprising that similar systems using elements metaphorically have been used in other cultures. The Chinese have for centuries used the five phases of energy transformation *wood, fire, earth, metal* and *water, which* places the human being in **a global context between** heaven and earth. The Chinese meridian system[1] which is narrowly linked to their system of the five phases of energy transformation, can tell us in great detail about the psychosomatic influences on our physical organs.

Footnote [1]) Energy channels throughout the body forming the bases for acupuncture and acupressure treatments

Anthroposophical medicine has investigated the connections between the planets and our physical organs, while the North American Indians developed a medicine wheel with reference to the four cardinal directions of North, South, East and West plus heaven and earth. Healing traditions in Tibet and India use our first four elements, adding like Paracelsus, the fifth element *space*. Placing ourselves in relationship with the basic aspects of existence, of the universe, of the myths of creation, connects us with a meaning in life and is a necessary framework for all healing work. We find this approach in sufism[1], in the various forms of shamanism[2] in Asia, Africa and America as well as in the Celtic tradition. Music, song and dance have played a role in all this since the beginnings of time. As different as these systems may appear to be, all of them teach us how we can **re-establish a harmony** with the world around us and God knows how badly we need to do this ! Therapy with the help of music and sounds works with the same approach and surely we are talking about the same harmony: In music as in life ?

Footnotes :
[1]) Islamic mysticism
[2]) a range of traditional beliefs and practices, that involve the ability to diagnose, cure illness because of a special relationship with, or control over, spirits. This tradition has existed all over the world since prehistoric times.

When listening, observing and proceeding to a qualitative musical evaluation we cannot limit ourselves simply to collecting logical and measurable criteria. Of course, these do have their function, but remain analytical and intellectual in nature, that is they are based in a left-brain activity. We also have to talk about feeling, musicality, intuition, access to the unconscious or preconscious layers. These are aspects of right brain activity which nowadays western science has great difficulty to integrate. Since music to a large extent activates the right hemisphere of the brain, music therapists cannot let themselves be disheartened by the cultural propensities to ignore right brain attributes. Fortunately, an increasing number of researchers and scientists have ventured into these right brain fields during the past two decades. Other cultures have done so for millennia. We are not alone.

The five elements form a progression from the most solid one – *earth* – to the most subtle – *space*. Conversely, coming from the element *space*, the elements get more and more solid. The Ancients tell us that this latter progression is exactly what brought about the creation of planet earth. The connections between the elements and the five lower energy centres relates each of them to a specific state of conscious-ness : *earth* to the physical level, *water* to the etheric layer, *fire* to the astral or emotional layer, *air* to mental consciousness and *space* to pure consciousness.

In music as in nature, the elements are always linked to each other. It is practically impossible to isolate one from another. For instance, earth may be *humid, cold, hot* or dry or it may have different combinations of these attributes such as *humid and cold* or *humid and hot*. Air can fan fire into life, when fire is strong enough; but if the fire is very small like a candle flame, air may extinguish it and the quality of fire will be changed. Let us not forget this interdependence while we look at the characteristics of each element.

Earth ☐

How can we hear and feel the element *earth* in someone's musical expression and how is it related to their psycho-energetic structure ? The feet and legs, the pelvic area and lower back including the kidneys have a direct link to the element *earth*. A good contact with these parts of our body brings us the necessary grounding. People who are too speedy, too cerebral lack contact with the earth and are often missing some stable basis in their life or a sense of personal success. Such people may find it very hard to trust themselves, to develop self-confidence and may often feel useless.

One of the reasons why such emotions arise is because those people have cut themselves off from their feelings and emotions. They create a blockage at the level of the diaphragm and the solar plexus. Their feelings and emotions get pushed down into the subconscious (*water*). The blockage interrupts the overall energy flow from head to feet and back again giving emotions too much power over thought processes and a person in this situation gets trapped in a vicious circle where the intellect is kept eternally busy through the interference of underlying emotions. Many of our so-called intellectual efforts are thus often being made under the influence of unacknowledged emotions.

Emotional shocks are experienced as a sort of earthquake inside us, that makes our knees and legs tremble. This weakens our contact with the *earth*. We can feel that someone is 'pulling the carpet from under our feet', a person may be considered as 'not having their feet on the ground' or having attitudes which 'are not down to earth' or they are people who 'cannot settle down'. Our spoken language acknowledges many links between our psycho-energetic functioning and the elements.

The basic qualities of the element *earth* are stability, permanence, heaviness and solidity – on a physical, mental and environmental level. Too much *earth* can result in wanting to sleep too much and in feeling heavy. Conversely if you have sleeping difficulties you may want to try the following exercise: while lying down in bed be very aware of your feet for some ten minutes and imagine yourself being covered by a warm layer of sand or fresh clean earth.

Each element influences the others and is influenced by them. We cannot isolate one from another. Earth generally contains some water. Water blends with earth and makes it fertile and malleable. If enough warmth (*fire*) is added and the earth is properly aired, everything will grow easily. On the contrary, if there is too much heat and not enough water, earth easily becomes a desert. *Earth* and *air* do not work well together. The wind can erode mountains, move dunes and blow away topsoil leaving barren land behind.

The earth element can take various symbolic forms. Each one will have its particular significance and will reveal a specific quality in our psycho-energetic makeup. It can take the form of a sandy beach, a dune, a stony desert, a rock, a mountain, a river bed, the foundations of a house, a cave suggesting a feminine, protective aspect, a freshly ploughed field, crystals or other precious stones indicating the influence of light or spiritual energy.

We often come into contact with animal symbols or with the energy of animals which live on or under the earth, snails, mice and suchlike. They too will tell us part of the client's personal story. Shamans, psychoanalysts and dream workers have throughout the ages drawn information from such symbols.

Everything that is an aspect of the **foundation of our lives** is linked to the *earth* element. Among these aspects are our connections with our bodies, our home, our work, our security, our successes, money, our relationships at home and at work. Past lives come into it as well. The symbol used for this element is the square, the most solid structure for a building's foundations as can be seen in the base of a pyramid. This symbol contains the number four which is found in the number of 'petals' of the root chakra, the energy centre at the base of our spine. Our DNA code, carrier of our genetic information, is formed only by four "letters" or basic elements. The Hartmann grid, named after the German geobiologist who discovered it, covers the entire earth with a grid of etheric energy lines, which are about 1.1 m apart. These energy lines form squares. The sense of smell is traditionally linked to the root chakra and brain scientists have revealed that the sense of smell, together with the sense of listening, are the first active senses in the unborn baby.

Our basic feelings about ourselves and the world around us often have their roots in early childhood, birth and pre-birth. Were we really wanted by our parents ? Did they have the means to truly accept us as we were ? Feeling accepted in those early stages of life is immensely helpful in our later expression. When non-acceptance is experienced the opposite situation is likely to arise and this may be at the origin of pathologies such as autism, psychotic states or other disharmonious evolutions. In the early history of an autistic child it is not rare to find the death of a parent or relative before or soon after his or her birth. If the adults close to the young child or unborn baby have been very emotional about the death and more particularly if the mother has been much absorbed by the event, the adults' attention may have been withdrawn from the unborn baby or infant for a number of weeks. This may have led the young being to feel abandoned for a period long enough to have affected the foundations of its life and through this his or her earth element. Marie Ainsworth, an English child psychiatrist underlines this in her scientific work. She has noted a number of personality profiles such as the 'secure' child with a stable base who is able to trust a motherly figure. However, in the absence of such a base an anxious, resistant or escaping child was the common result (Ainsworth et al., 1978).

In order to ground our thoughts and to be able to concentrate we need a good contact with the element *earth*. When our mental energy is not well anchored, it accumulates around the head area and slips out of our control. The reason for this is very often an interruption in the overall circulation of energy that should bring the energy down from the head to the feet and up again. Our feeling contact with strong emotions can be blocked at the solar plexus and the diaphragm in the *fire* area making it impossible for us to 'digest' the emotions. In other words, we do not experience them in our belly region. When we improve our earth contact our mental energy can again take part in the overall flow of energy and this will include a conscious approach to our emotions. In musical expression a client will then be able, maybe for the first time in many years, to play continuously on one musical instrument for several minutes. Even if she were able to play for only twenty seconds, this may sometimes reveal a significant positive change.

We may want to consider how we take care of the *earth* itself. I feel the whole question of recycling or burying waste into the *earth*, surface mining, covering large surfaces with concrete and many other issues affect the *earth* element as a whole. This is not to be taken lightly and the consequences may very well be starting to be felt quite dramatically.

I like Matthew Fox's[1] way of linking the root chakra to our capacity to feel connected to the All-there-is, to the Cosmos. Through our contact with the *earth* we do in fact come into contact with all creation. This chakra links us simultaneously to earth and heaven (Fox, 2000).

Footnote :
[1]) author and reviver of the tradition of creation spirituality

When trying to activate someone's earth connection while playing music, we might choose a **musical instrument** that needs to be played standing up, such as a large drum. In so doing we are encouraging the person to breathe deeply down into their belly. This may start to soften a possible blockage in the diaphragm. Listening to a didgeridoo, large gongs and deep singing voices while directing our attention to the lower part of our bodies can also help this softening process. I am convinced that a therapist can only help a client gain a better grounding, if he himself is well grounded. Good grounding needs a constant effort. Deficient grounding is rarely improved in one or two days.

There are awareness exercises to improve one's contact with the earth. These exercises direct our attention to our feet so as to link our feet with the root chakra and sometimes also the pineal chakra at the forehead. For example, an exercise may combine slow deep breathing with movements such as shifting the body weight from one foot to the other in a repetitive rocking motion. In doing an exercise like this it is very important that our intention, of directing our thoughts to our left food i.e., is followed by our feeling perception of what we observe when doing so.

The musical elements which help to improve one's contact with the earth and which give one a feeling of security are musical **structures** that consist of slow regular rhythms, a drone sound and minimalist style patterns. If you attach ribbons hung with small bells to a child's ankles, this will automatically draw the child's attention to his feet. Obviously massaging feet and legs, having hot foot baths and visualising one's feet buried in warm sand or earth, will improve one's earth contact.

Everyone has key thought structures which are the foundation of one's being and beliefs. If beliefs are not based on personal experience and personal convictions, they will not be properly grounded. If such thought structures and beliefs are questioned, challenged or modified, one may experience an emotional earthquake.

Let us remember here the mountain example mentioned earlier. The quality of a *mountain* is a symbol for the earth element. Opposite to the *mountain* quality is the quality of a *valley*. The *mountain* represents male qualities including stability, steadiness, solitude. At its summit the mountain has a connection to space and silence. The *valley* represents female qualities and is associated with movement, velocity, most rivers as well as roads and train lines are found in valleys, and with social life. When we wish to express a mountain musically, we need to contact the mountain qualities inside us and to strengthen them. If someone finds it difficult to imagine *earth* or a *mountain* and cannot feel connected to them, she must be allowed some time to become familiar with the image, to feel its qualities, to become aware of possible obstacles towards its expression within herself and to dissolve them.

That is the therapeutic or human growth dimension in this work with the five elements. It is necessary to bring feelings and expression into a balance, into a kind of osmotic relationship where the feelings flow unfiltered into the expression. Engaging with the elements in their natural conditions teaches us all we need to know. It is far more interesting to do this than to read about it in print which is why I shall now stop writing about the *earth*.

Working suggestions
Let the person you are working with play stable structures, a drone for instance, let her keep a steady rhythm, using their body while playing the instrument, beating a drum for instance. Check that the player is breathing deeply into the belly. You may tie ribbons hung with small bells around their ankles. Encourage the player to stamp their feet rhythmically and to play and dance bare footed.

Water

The *water* area extends from the pelvic area upwards to just underneath the navel. This is the area of the body with the highest percentage of water and with few bones, except for the spine. In this *water* area we find the hara, a main energy centre and the centre of gravity in the human body. Accordingly, this energy centre has great significance in Tai Chi and in all martial arts. The hara is strongly associated with our **instinctive intelligence**. Water cleanses and connects us to the elimination processes of our body.

The half-moon symbol opening upwards forms a vessel able to receive water. The moon has a very particular link to water as the tidal movements reveal. Let us not forget the strong symbolic association between the moon and our subconscious which contrasts sharply with the symbolic association between the sun and our consciousness. The prone half-moon draws our attention to its lowest point, a point of balance, for example between the male and female aspects in each of us, and a centre of gravity.

When we look at the four layers of the etheric, we find a complementarity between water whose symbol is a semicircle and air whose symbol is a full circle. (See also explanations on the energy fields in chapter one). The 'chemical ether', the innermost layer of the etheric field corresponding to the *water* element, will become incapable of nourishing our body's cells if the link with the outermost layer of the etheric, the 'reflector ether' corresponding to the *air* element, is not maintained. Matthew Fox too underlines the unifying aspect of water, the cup symbol and the hara chakra. This chakra unifies the opposed male and female principles and links with the 'feminist philosophy', according to his 'creation spirituality'. Water and air are considered to be feminine energies in ancient Indian wisdom, earth and fire as masculine energies.

The *earth* element, as already described, is symbolised by the mountain, the male triangle pointing upwards, whereas the element *water* can be symbolised by the valley, the female triangle pointing downwards. This triangle has the shape of a valley. Valleys receive spring waters, brooks and rivers and have themselves the quality of movement, of velocity, whereas mountains are stable and unmoving.

> The Spirit of the valley never dies.
> It is the mysterious female.
> The mysterious female knows
> The passage leading to Heaven and Earth
> Dimly visible,
> We guess its presence
> Yet use will never drain it.
>
> Lao Tse, Tao Te King, verse 6

The water area of the body is inseparable from the etheric energy field and its **subconscious memory**. This part of our psycho-energetic system is the key to our vitality, our sexuality and our creativity and it can be characterised in its emotional dimension with the energy of anger, which is nothing other than the suppression of our vital aspects. Someone who lives fully these natural aspects is usually calm, peaceful and is well connected to his body and sexuality. His movements and thoughts will be harmonious and *fluid*. He will be flexible and playful.

An ancient Indian philosophical tradition describes a progression of the five elements in the creation process of our world, starting with the element *space* or *ether* the least material element, finishing with the element *earth* the most dense and solid element. In the Indian tradition of thought each element is created by the previous element. *Fire* brings about an expansion that leads to a progressive cooling which will bring forth *water*. So, *water* becomes the creative base of all physical manifestation, *earth*. If these thoughts seem strange us, we can remind ourselves how we were created in water, the amniotic fluid in our mother's womb. The myth of creation in the Hebrew bible follows the same steps. This may explain why the *water* area plays such a key role in our creative capacities.

Obstructions in the *water* area are not only apparent in body language but can also be recognised at a **symbolic level**. In a person's dreams, as well as in his imagination, water would then show itself in the form of ice, frost or snow and being hardened would not be able to move freely anymore. These symbols of frozen, immobile water may be reflecting someone's rigid thought patterns and constrained body movements. Such a person might intuitively perceive stagnant water or a dam, maybe one about to burst, as well as images of sharks or crocodiles. Images of sea monsters may appear and these will be pointing out subconscious fears and aggressive thoughts. These fears may not only be revealed by the state of the water itself, but also by what is under the surface of the water. This is a familiar metaphor for our subconscious often used in fairy tales. Autistic people, for instance, have an ambiguous relationship to water and so to their own body. They may go through phases of intense fear about water, but may also be fascinated by the sound of running water in pipes for example, as if instinctively recognising their need to integrate this aspect.

We should carefully note images, impressions or dreams which present metallic structures associated with water. Such images symbolise the excessive interference by rigid thoughts in the water area. In this case the movements of the person will often be jerky rather than fluid suggesting lack of tonicity and control. Such a person may beat a drum too violently without realising it, so I would usually take away any beater from the player and let her strike the drum with her bare hands. She would then become more aware of the violence within through the pain in her hands.

It is through the condition of the *water* element that we may better understand the mechanisms leading to **fascism**. Fascism is an opposing force to creativity. Fascist style education – still present to a greater or lesser degree in many families and schools and still widely considered to be a very efficient way of rearing children– is characterised by a lack of respect for the individual's needs marked by an insistence on obedience to external authority. This will more specifically have an influence on a person's *water* aspect. To encourage the unfolding of a person's creativity and individuality is very important. If we do this there will be fewer adolescent suicides, less depression and misuse of drugs that themselves bring about the suffocation of vitality and creativity.

To be of lasting benefit all transformation of the energy in an energy centre needs an influx of spiritual energy, energy that comes from beyond the emotional and mental levels. The inferior and destructive aspects of the hara chakra, the centre of the water area, such as anger, violence, sexuality, instinctive drives, fascist tendencies and subconscious influences, need to be placed under the control of the higher mental and spiritual aspects which are linked to an individual's quality aspects. It is obvious that beating on a drum only will not do the job. Hence the necessity, once someone desires a real transformation, for engaging in personal development through disciplined work with awareness exercises.

On a musical level the element *water* can be expressed through the capacity to move fluently and playfully from one musical idea to the next, through **lively and ever-changing rhythms**. The rhythm of water is different from a mere regular pulsation. Pulsation and unchanging rhythmical patterns belong to the *earth* element because they create stable *structures* and are *bases* for any musical development. When we see a river or a brook from an aeroplane, we notice that it characteristically meanders, revealing to us this natural movement of living rhythms. A river that is prevented from flowing naturally loses its capacity to cleanse its own bed.

Large, soft **hand drums**, whose skin is not stretched too tight, frame drums such as the Irish bodhran or the North African bendhir, talking drums, clay pot drums such as the Nigerian oudou or Indian ghatam seem particularly appropriate instruments to help people access the element *water*. The physical effort required to play them is of course also helpful. To maintain a rhythm, you must integrate it into your body's memory, the subconscious memory, and be able to play it from the hara, to play it from your guts. Traditional Chinese Medicine has for centuries been suggesting drumming to help what they call the phase of energy transformation water and its natural link to the kidneys. The rain stick, the ocean drum and recordings of the sound of water, whether of waves at the sea shore, brooks, wells or rainfall, can be very useful in this context.

Trance like rituals, based on dance and rhythms, have often been used as a means to restore balance in the *water* area. The different musical genres such as rap, techno, reggae and African music are a big comeback for rhythm. The fashionable djembes or other trance inducing instruments such as the didgeridoo, document the search in our own culture and the difficulties it presents, to re-establish a natural contact with the element *water*. However, if the trance inducing ritual includes too much hard metallic playing, often present in techno music, the conflict between hard jerkiness and fluidity will appears. I believe it is important to emphasise the conscious aspect in trance dance and respect for individuality in contrast to group or mass rituals and movements where individual expression is neglected.

Someone's *water* quality can be observed through the intermediary of involuntary associations, images, watery feelings and aquatic animals. This perception engages the right hemisphere of the brain and is therefore not logical or analytical in nature so it may take a bit of practice. It is **a soft, peripheral observation,** as though watching from the corner of your eyes, which will lead you into this kind of feeling listening. The details of internal images can be quite eloquent. All have their particular significance. Not only do they provide information on the nature of a person's particular problem, but also on her own healing potential, ready to be activated. As in all therapeutic work, we need to distinguish between our own projections, that is interference by our own emotions, and what is really happening within the patient.

Musical improvisations guided by imagery through instructions given in advance or during playing can be very helpful in the process. We can for instance suggest to someone to move out of some stagnant water towards clean running water. Suggesting the image of a dolphin, a whale or a seahorse can help someone to enter the depths beneath the water's surface. One can also be helped – why not – by imagining the sun's rays lighting up the underwater world. It is always very surprising to recognise with what precision such an image brings about the feeling of an element in the quality of the music played or sung. Sometimes when working with a group of people I would whisper an image to two or three participants for them to express in their improvisation. Often, I let the other participants listen, respond to their feelings and draw. The concordance between their drawings and the original whispered image, unknown to them, is very often unexpected. A task like this cannot be carried out using our logical brain. What is required is the musicians' feeling capacity, their spontaneous, uncensored expression.

Working with **visualisations** or images popping up from the subconscious is very similar to working with dream interpretation. At first, when someone connects with her imaginative capacity and feels or sees images coming up from inside, she may be quite faint. This stage can evolve quite quickly and other aspects may come in. One thing that fascinates me is that beyond the person's primary focus on a fore ground scene, she can access a wealth of information in her peripheral vision. You may ask her questions about the surrounding circumstances, such as the weather, the light conditions, the landscape behind her; whether there are any animals or persons present; what is happening behind her back, what is the feeling of the scene ? The person will often be able to answer those questions with certainty. Knowing exactly where objects or persons are in the scenery or what shades of colour are present is also most significant. Is the little brook on her left or right hand side ? Imagined scenes and images are not composed at random. They are very precise and if it is necessary lend themselves to detailed interpretation.

Some very astonishing encounters can happen. During one course I suggested that participants lie down and let themselves be carried away by the drum music I was playing. At one moment I had the impression of a very gentle wild animal approaching the scene and walking around us silently. Then it seemed to sit down next to a woman and remained there looking away from her. Normally I would let such an impression pass without attaching too much importance to it at the particular moment. What surprised me was the woman's account of her own experience. She had felt the paws of a light animal walking all over her belly, then over her chest area, as if a large cat had climbed over her.

Another time, during a course I gave in Copenhagen, I suggested to a woman of about sixty to launch into a free improvisation using one of the easy instruments placed in the middle of the group circle (see list of instruments at the end of the book). She chose an African mbira or thumb piano. Instead of plucking its fine blades she turned it upside down and started to slap on it with the palm of her hand. The instrument started to resonate with all its blades. Within a very few seconds an intense atmosphere was established. I then had the strong impression that this woman was at that very moment completely in tune with nature. It felt to me as though she was surrounded by the kind of tundra you can find in the far north. I felt the presence of a large animal. I could not tell whether or not it was an elk. I just knew he was big. When she had finished playing, we shared our observations and impressions. Someone briefly talked about an elephant then stopped.

After that the woman who had played so beautifully told us something that had happened to her several months ago. She was woken up once in the middle of the night by what she felt was the trumpeting of an elephant. She was living somewhere in the Danish countryside and so she thought that it was somewhat embarrassing to hear a distant elephant somewhere in Denmark far away from any town. Next morning, she got a phone call from her son who told her that he had just been sitting with his son on a beach somewhere else in Denmark, when a small elephant had approached them from behind. This had given the little boy a wonderful thrill.

This series of coincidences could easily be discarded as being haphazard and unworthy of attention. But in the context of this way of working, there was no sense in not considering them for a moment. Why had three persons in the group reported a similar impression, especially in the context of Denmark ? I was convinced that there was important information in all of this especially for the woman concerned. I gave her my impression, telling her that I felt she had a great sensitivity which she had to take seriously, that she had a rare gift of tuning into nature and the animal world. Such a gift was seldom used in our days and it was very likely that she could use this gift for the benefit of other people. It was most likely that she needed to express this gift which would also take her a step further along her own path.

Let us come back to water. Harmonisation in our *water* dimension only happens when we bring our male and female sides into a better balance, that is balancing feelings and expression, instinctual and rational responses, emotional and mental states. Improving deep belly breathing will help to bring about this balance, as will massage and dance for both of these connect us to rhythm. People who avoid these aspects of their *water* element suppress essential and vital parts of their being and are very likely to get trapped in subconscious vicious emotional circles that can get quite out of control. People suffering from schizophrenia are conspicuous victims of these mechanisms. Their etheric aspect is considerably enlarged in the water area of their body. This suggests that they are hiding their emotions out of sight of their consciousness and away from their physical reality. Suppressed expression contains emotional energy and the subconscious memory as well as the thought structures connected with this. It is often held in the body around the thighs, hips and pelvic area – that is the '*water*' area.

Personal development seeks an overall harmonisation, that is to say a natural balance between all the different levels within us. None of the levels should be discarded, so working on our *water* aspect is a complex matter. It is associated with work on the hara chakra of course. The words 'chakra' and 'energy' are unfortunately often used by people who have no idea of the complexity involved in those phenomena. This often results in promises being given to balance or heal all the chakra centres in one weekend, which is a completely unrealistic promise. It is not as easy as that. Here I have underlined the multidimensional nature of the subject and anyone who has undertaken serious work on any chakra and the different problems presented in so doing knows this. The difficult things are to become aware of one's own blind spots and dead ends, to learn a set of exercises and to generate the will to practice them conscientiously so as to illuminate and clarify these difficulties.

Working on our *water* element can take our development a long way. We may start with wanting to overcome our fear of water, or wanting to become aware of our resistance to imagining any space below the surface, perhaps because of the crocodiles or other sea monsters we might meet down there. Even establishing a balance between our male and female aspects is quite an achievement. It often takes time. It is very often an initiation where 'the path is the goal', which is to say that the disciplined 'walking along' towards the desired result is all that counts. It is especially important when working on one's water aspect to slowly dissolve all hardness towards oneself, remembering that it is just this hardness of thought interference that disturbs the rhythm of *water*, the rhythm of life. This hardness is often symbolised in images of ice, snow, dams and all kinds of metal structures appearing in or near water.

Take a short moment to reflect on what we humans have done to **our rivers**. Intensive agriculture whose heavy tractors have compressed and compacted the *earth*, has at the same time created vast fields with no hedges or other brakes where rain water now runs down very fast with little time to soak into the ground. This, together with deforestation is one of the reasons for recent world-wide spectacular floods. Like all the other elements comprising our planet, the *water* element is out of balance.

On a symbolic level, **dreams** of huge tidal waves usually announce something 'big' from the subconscious surfacing into consciousness in the near future. We had better prepare ourselves for this, watching our dreams, doing some extra grounding exercises and working on a good body contact. To understand the natural way of water we need only pour a jug of water onto some outdoor tiles. Water will always find a way out which eventually will bring it back to union with the ocean. In the course of finding its way, water shows considerable creativity and ingenuity.

Musical expression helps the inner development work provided one proceeds with gentleness and takes the time required.

Working suggestions
Does the patient or pupil express his or her vitality ? Does she or he have access musically to their female aspect, left side, left hand, left foot and to their male side right side, hand and foot? Can she move

fluently from one musical idea to the next or does she get stuck with a single idea? Are her actions hard, abrupt or violent? Does she mistreat the instruments ?

Slow uneven rhythms of say three, five or seven beats seem to me to be especially helpful in bringing about a better contact with the belly area. These rhythms lead to a natural swaying of the body from side to side to emphasise the beat which alternates from side to side continuously.

Guided imagery with the little brook
W. a woman in her thirties had some difficulties in contacting her *water* area. She felt quickly overwhelmed by destructive, angry emotions. It seemed evident to me that she concealed an underlying pain that she needed to release. She had in fact had several abortions whose pains of various kinds she had not completely let go of. In the pauses during the workshop I often saw her playing on the balafon in a dreamy way, with little intensity. I asked her later on to go to the balafon and play a little river. Her playing was quite mechanical and needed more playfulness, while intensity was still missing. I suggested that she imagine more water coming down in that little river, to let the water flow around strongly, jumping over the stones in the riverbed. Seeing that she still could not invest herself fully in the activity, I suggested she tried again more playfully by imagining a leaf being carried down by the flowing water, or a child's little paper boat bouncing along. Her play became more intense. Then I suggested that she imagine rays of sunlight penetrating the surface of the water, illuminating the stones down in the riverbed. Her play became lighter but still not free flowing like a babbling brook.

My next idea was to ask her to let the river reach the shore of a little lake and to allow her attention to glide under the surface of the water so as to explore its depth. She said she felt more and more surrounded by darkness, yet at the same time she was feeling more secure. Her playing mirrored her experience. It felt deeper and more assured. The mechanical aspect present in her playing at the start had completely gone. She felt ready to meet some hidden aspects of her *water* element. The following night she dreamed that she was sitting on a toilet losing a lot of blood from her womb. This seemed to be a clear symbol of her willingness to acknowledge and to let go some of her painful personal history. During the previous days we had all worked with energy exercises designed to bring more light and clarity into the area below the navel. As so often happens, it was the combination of concentration of thought and feeling awareness that brought about the depth of work one can reach through musical expression.

Fire

The symbol for the *fire* element is a triangle pointing upwards, a male triangle. It reminds us of the prism that allows light to be separated into its component colours. It reminds us also of the bottom level with its two opposite aspects and the third one, the controlling aspect being on a higher level, the top of the triangle.

For most of us, using the analytical left hemisphere of our brain presents no difficulty. However, because we use it so commonly, we often have great difficulty in recognising and responding to the other, more intuitive right hemisphere of our brain. This is surprising because music does stimulate the brain's right hemisphere very well. Music arouses all our feeling aspects. One part of the explanation for the unbalanced use of our brain's two hemispheres is associated with our contact to our personal *fire* element as well as to our culture's general attitude to the fire element.

Should we not include in our understanding of the fire element the way our societies characteristically handle fire. We permit nuclear power installations, the manufacture of military fire arms and weapons of all kinds, the burning of fossil fuels, there are more suicidal actions with explosives, terrorist attacks using explosives and more forest fires in recent years. Parallel to all this have we not banned fire from our homes and towns : fewer and fewer fire places, the Christmas tree's candles changed into electric light bulbs. Did this happen by chance ? We are afraid of fire. Fear is precisely the emotion that is linked to the *fire* area. There is of course a strong link between the mechanisms of fear and anger. The first reaction to getting flooded by other people's emotions is fear (or its opposites love and understanding). Feeling fear then often generates anger if the person has access to the hara, since the power of anger comes from the belly are, the hara.

The *fire* area of the body lies between the navel and the lower end of the sternum. When we speak of *fire*, we are talking about transformation, be it on a digestive level in heartburn, in dreams or in emotional experiences. We may also experience a burning sensation in the solar plexus area when we wake up from a nightmare which presented us with intensely fearful and bewildering situations.

The energy centre at the **solar plexus** is where other people's emotions enter into us. Someone who has not learned how to protect himself well enough may be smothered by these incoming emotions which are often very powerful. Consequently, sooner or later, most of us will try to cut off our experience of these emotions by blocking our breathing at the solar plexus level. This prevents the painful experiences of these emotions from descending into the belly and guts, which act as a sort of resonance box for emotions. If we feel fearful of and threatened by other people's reactions, a common experience in childhood, when we want to express our own feelings, we start to numb our awareness of our emotional experiences. In spite of doing this, the emotions will continue to be active but will remain in the subconscious, beyond conscious control. This can be the foundation of a constant, uncontrollable feeling of fear of being overwhelmed by yet more emotions.

People who are dominated by fear lack warmth in their expression, they stay cool. Unfortunately, these defence mechanisms can establish themselves rather early in life and they may bring about a slowing down or an underdevelopment in the development of certain centres in the brain, especially in the frontal lobe. This often allows serious behavioural troubles to take hold, autism, psychosis and other pervasive development disorders for example. The navel with its obvious link to the prenatal and postnatal period is part of the *fire* area. We can readily distinguish four collective fears : fear of sexuality, fear of mental illness, fear of physical illness and fear of death. This gives us quite a range of themes to work with when dealing with the *fire* element. The basic transformation of emotions happens when we can accept who we are with our entire personal history, our weaknesses *and* our strengths.

Fire is essential to **transform** emotions into feelings. The opposite experience to fear is **love**, **understanding** and **acceptance**. There is a strong link between the astral field and the solar plexus centre. The transforming *fire* element also brings about ripening and maturation which are transformation processes.

When an energy blockage in the lower area of the body is dissolved a wave of heat may be generated. Like all other heat forms it will rise up through the body. Transforming emotions releases energy which can be used in the heart centre, that is in the *air* area of the body. This is discussed below. *Fire* also brings us into contact with **light**. This is a very important component in the transformation process, since *light* is linked to the influx of spiritual energy. Thus, *fire* brings about moments of light and hope. It is light that enables us to see objects around us and which symbolically reveals to us a direction for our life (Satyasangananda, 2000).

In the evolutionary conception of the elements it is *air* that is the origin of *fire*. Consciousness perceives objects for the first time and becomes aware of itself, realising that it is a separate entity. In Indian philosophical tradition this phase corresponds to the onset of ego, the sense of a separate, enduring self. It is not surprising, therefore, that there are strong links between the solar plexus centre, the sense of sight, the ego, emotions, the lower mental field and its emotional and intellectual content. The lower mental field can be widely infiltrated by emotions and can be used to block emotional experiences. Our sense of sight can be disturbed at times by what is happening in the solar plexus. Sometimes our sight becomes blurred when we look into someone else's eyes. This can be a clear sign that there are emotions present affecting the solar plexus area and that some confusion is about.

We can quite easily detect in someone's musical expression a poor contact with his *fire* element. The musical expression is stale, superficial, foggy, boring, perhaps lacking structure or being too rigid. Do not forget that a deficiency in one element may very well cause an imbalance in the other elements. Wellbeing is all a matter of balance and inter-connectedness. When someone's expression lacks warmth and radiation, listening to her playing does not warm our hearts. "If we are dominated by fire, for example, then we try to activate water or earth, and vice versa. If earth is dominant – we are dull, sleepy, heavy – then we activate air or fire. And if air dominates us – we are flighty, nervous, with a short attention span – then we activate earth or water." (Wangyal, 2002, p.22).

Daily life is full of examples of this constant search for balance, we drink water when we are dry, hot and thirsty, we cool ourselves with cold, wet flannels when we are feverish. The weather, certain emotions and thoughts, what we eat, an illness, a draft of air, people we meet, noise, pollution, almost anything can cause an imbalance in the elements or conversely can help us to restore them to balance.

While the element 'earth' can be seen in musical structures, *water* will be recognised by lively, slightly ever-changing rhythms, *fire* will be heard in the dynamic aspects of music changing volume from soft to loud. We will feel *fire* through the **warmth** and the **radiation** in expression. Therapeutic work on a large drum, using one's voice, or playing on a cymbal, small metallic percussion or a gong can be very beneficial, providing one is not forcing and is staying connected to one's feelings. It is interesting to see how many people who have unresolved problems in the solar plexus feel irritable and even attacked by these metallic sounds.

On an imaginary level we can suggest to someone to imitate a lion's roar, to play the fire spitting dragon or to imitate lightning and thunder. As soon as the person has integrated that dimension, then we can suggest to her to express warmth, radiation, a sunrise, the gentle warmth of a candle, a fire's embers, the warm sand we may lie down on. Using our imagination is a very important aspect for any intuitive observation. It is one part of our feelings, of our brain's right hemisphere's perception.

When we become accustomed to noting how our everyday language refers to the elements, to noting other people's quality of expression and when we let ourselves develop a feeling awareness of these phenomena, the suggested parallels will become clearer and more obvious. The mechanisms of the solar plexus are complex and especially so because some of our fears are actually deeply rooted. Consequently, our automatic reactions will often be ruled by prejudices. Our mental defence mechanisms are subtle as revealed in some of our thinking habits and we should not underestimate them, neither in ourselves nor in others. How often do we let habits and fears govern our communications rather than letting love and generosity express themselves ? Our emotional structures have their own intelligence and are inclined to resist when we want to change them. The transformation work with the *fire* element needs continuous effort.

Interpreting the symbols for fire that appear in our **dreams** can be very useful. Fire can destroy and in so doing may transform matter towards a non-material form. It is a catalyst that brings about change, renewal and evolution. Like *earth fire* is a male or positive energy electrically speaking. Water and air are female, absorbent or negative energies. The images in our subconscious tell us whether we are in a process of purification and real change or whether our inner *fire* is being smothered. In order to control *fire* in a productive sense we need the help of the element *earth* as a container and to provide strength and fuel together with *water* to cool it, to extinguish it or at least slow it down if necessary. *Fire* also needs *air* to stimulate it.

Observing the parallels with real fire is revealing. To contain an open air fire we would build a stone circle around it and at home we use a hearth or a fire place (*earth*). Even electricity (*fire*) is run through wires (*earth*). Studying the elements in their natural conditions helps us to understand how to balance them within us.

Working suggestions
Is the person afraid of certain types of sound ? Could this indicate an excessive vulnerability in the solar plexus area and the nervous system ? Is she showing warmth in her expression ? Does she have the tendency to want to control everything because she fears feeling empty and powerless because of her lack of creativity and inability to feel her emotions ? We can try using the 'lion's roar', 'the dragon's rage', 'thunder and lightening', or 'the candle's light', 'fanning the embers into life 'a baking oven', 'the heating', 'a sunrise or sunset', 'a warm beach'.

Instruments which can help the player to access his *fire* element are xylophones and the African balafon (both when played with hard mallets), wood blocks, castanets, foot rattles, bell ribbons, maracas, guiro, chascas, cymbals, singing bowls, bells, gongs, drums, clapsticks. Using the voice is also quite an effective instrument for working on the *fire* aspect.

Working with *fire* can help someone find the gateway into emotions stored away in the bottom areas of the body, *water* and *earth*. I have worked with a boy in music therapy who always felt tired after only ten minutes or so. He got in touch with his vitality and creativity for the first time in music therapy only when I insisted on working for a while with *fire* on a big drum while he used his voice at the same time. That day he started to use his whole body while playing.

Air

The symbol for the air element is a circle which has throughout the ages been used as a symbol for unity, for the All-There-Is, the Universe, the Spiritual dimension. The *air* zone in our body corresponds to our chest area including the lungs and the heart. The *air* element and the lungs are involved in exchanges between the inner and the outer, the near and the far, above and below, spirit and matter, myself and others. The element *air* links everything, puts everything into relationship and is concerned with different kinds of communication. It allows the spirit to see things from a different angle by stepping back a bit, by looking from a bird's eye view. It is scarcely surprising, therefore, that the *air* element and the heart chakra are our doors to the spiritual dimension, to greater freedom, to compassion and to our eternal source.

This air area is very sensitive to **the spiritual dimension in our lives**. When we neglect it depression is not far away. We feel a weight on our chest. The human immune system is under the influence of the thymus gland found just behind the sternum. Its effectiveness depends very much on a good balance in the *air* element. The root of the word 'thymus' is in the ancient Greek word '*thumos*' which means 'seat of passion'. So, the air zone is related to what we feel passionate about, what makes us tick. In the Tibetan Buddhist tradition *air* provides us with the necessary speed to rapidly change an emotion into its positive feeling aspect.

Can we hear and sense the *air* element in musical expression ? Can we detect a player who is depressed or weighed down ? The *air* element knows two extremes, the manic state or 'high pressure' in meteorological language and depression or 'low pressure'. The soaring movements in a melody, the lightness in a person's playing can make us feel the presence of the element *air*. Musical instruments that can help someone to find access to his *air* element are flutes and the monochord which I write about further on. Singing and using our arms and hands in accompaniment to music can also be very useful.

In general, all music instruments that are designed to express **melodies** will facilitate contact with the air element such as the violin, piano, keyboard and accordion. Brass instruments predictably influence the *fire* area. Metal percussion instruments do have a strong connection to the *air* area and the mental aura that starts at the heart (see chapter one). Traditional Chinese medicine recommends working with gongs, bells, singing bowls and tubular bells for the metal/lungs area which corresponds in this respect with our air element. Metallic sounds trigger a natural expansion of consciousness.

The flute is a wind instrument and those who play it always risk to some extent, if they are not careful, losing their earth contact, or grounding, when playing it. There is a tendency to 'fly off', to cut oneself off from one's feet and legs. You can sometimes detect this in a flautist's playing. While listening to flute playing, we might start to feel woozy. The musician's playing can become too airy. She may get lost in the space. We play who we are.

An imbalance in this part of our psycho-energetic system can come from thought structures rooted in early childhood. This early period of life can especially affect the upper chest area between the level of the nipples and the collar bones, which area includes the thymus gland. The death of a close person, if inadequately mourned will also have an effect on the same area. Feeling sorry for oneself or getting into a depressive withdrawal may well be tactics employed by the *air* element. Expressions of joy and compassion would be the antidote to these tactics. It is essential to free oneself from anything that weighs heavily on one's heart such as the stress, resentment and bitterness that one may hold on to after having been deceived.

Many emotions such as hatred or feeling rejected, even though first affecting other areas of the body, will eventually end up affecting the heart chakra and the physical heart. In such a condition we will feel weighed down and depressed and will certainly find it difficult to be carried away by our dreams and in*spir*ations. The words 'inspiration' and 'aspiration' reminds us that the Latin root *'spirare'* relates to breathing, both in the physical and symbolic sense.

In order to **transform the emotions** held onto in this area of the body and in the psycho-energetic system we must call upon *spir*itual energy. There are two subtle channels for incoming inspiration that meet at the heart chakra. They originate beyond our energy fields, approaching us over the collar bones. I noticed these lines in a Tibetan thangka picturing the medicine Buddha. Tanka[1]. They form a female triangle where the lowest point is at the heart chakra. This inspirational movement is the necessary counterpart to the transformation of emotions, a process that finishes at the heart chakra. Inspirations are actually felt in the heart area. The thymus gland that is thought by the western conventional medical profession to atrophy at puberty, does so only if it does not get adequate spiritual energy.

Footnote :
[1] a Tibetan religious painting on fabric

'Air' is in continuous movement. Movement, *fluctuations*, accelerations, slowing down and melodies are the musical clues to this element. We talk about melodies that 'carry us away', that 'uplift us', that 'raise our spirits', that 'give us wings'. Melodies invite us, like no other musical component, to raise our arms and hands in readiness for the dance. Hands and the sense of touch are closely connected to the heart chakra. We quickly realize it if a certain musical interpretation gives us a sense of freedom and lightness, or conversely if it evokes heavy sensations in us and we do not experience uplifting feelings. We soon know whether a player is giving us a sense of deep joy and inspiration or if she is just rousing our superficial reactions. Even when the title to a piece may associate itself with the *air* element, this may be nothing more than a good intention.

Birds, most particularly eagles, and big sailing boats are two other important symbols for the *air* element. They remind us of our deep connections to the sky, to heaven and to the distant shores of the land of our dreams. We feel that the bird is symbolically closer to the Divine. The bird represents the messenger between the lower and higher dimensions of existence. We may sometimes envy them because they have a wide overview of the scenes below them. Who has not felt the need to rise above daily worries so as to get back to the essentials of existence ? The symbol of the flying bird relates to the two elements *air* and *space*.

Working suggestions
Does the person feel light-hearted, does she take wing when she plays and moves? Is there melodic and harmonic sensitivity in her playing, a sense of beauty, of joy ? Does she have a pattern of depressive withdrawals ?
Ask the person to play the 'eagle', 'the wind', 'fast spiralling movements of air and leaves in autumn' or 'a feather that gently glides down to earth'.

Space

How can we be more aware of '*space*' than when it is absent? People who are continuously busy and in an agitated state and who always seem to want to produce noise on an instrument, who cannot grant themselves or others any moment of silence, these are the people who lack *space*. They have not found their true centre. *Space* is an obvious quality which surrounds us on a mountain top or when we are gazing up into the vast blue sky. We can experience it when walking across a large plain, when watching the surface of a big lake or staring at the horizon. In such situations we can let ourselves sink into *space*, be absorbed by it while feeling it within us too. The element *space* reminds us of consciousness, of the spirit with no beginning and no end.

The circle symbol has that same quality. The space circle symbol has a dot in the middle which stands for consciousness. Like the structure of an atom, there is *space* between the dot and the outer circle. *Space* has neither colour nor shape and yet at the same time nothing exists without it. We should not forget that on the atomic level as well as in the universe itself *space* is the predominant element. Between the electrons and the nucleus of an atom there is an immense space.

This element brings us to the field of meditation, the experience of silence, the capacity to simply be. *Space*, sometimes called *ether*, fills everything between people, between objects. Moreover, it allows what takes place between people. Sound is carried by the ether. The two opposed states of the element *space* are expression and suppression.

The Tibetans say : he who masters this element, knows the nature of spirit. He knows the essential and does not search on the outside in order to find the cause of his problems. Seeing them arise in space, he does not identify with them anymore (Wangyal, 2002). That is why in the Tibetan traditions of Tantra and Dzogchen *space* is considered to be the true centre.

The journey towards experiencing this element fully brings us mental space, stillness and opens up new horizons. Buddhists call it emptiness, the essence of spirit. This wisdom is held by many indigenous people who have kept alive this sacred link to their origins. "Silence is the absolute balance of body, spirit and soul. People who can preserve this unity of being stay forever calm, untouched by the storms of existence" (Ohiyesa Indian, quotation from *lettre d'information No. 8 of the French association Tchendukua, March 2003*, an association that helps the Kogi Indians in Columbia to restore their rituals and to get back some of their land).

The body area that is especially associated with this element of *space* lies between the upper end of the chest bone and the bridge of the nose, so including the thyroid chakra, the ears, the mouth, the vocal cords and the point of silence at the bridge of the nose.

The Indian philosophical tradition notes that sound cannot travel in a void, so it is the *space* or *ether* element that provides the necessary medium for the movement of sound. The yogic tradition reminds us that it is this element that allows us to control our emotions. For when this element is active our consciousness moves away from its attachment to the sensual world. The active presence of this element is a prerequisite for any spiritual development or growth of mind.

To express *space,* we need a good contact with the first four elements and the ability to transform the emotions associated with each chakra and each body zone. Our voice is an excellent witness to this process. Just as all our physical tensions are reflected in our neck, the thyroid energy centre will reflect all imbalances in the four lower chakras : root, hara, solar plexus and heart.

The qualities of space and silence are rare ingredients in western music. However, towards the end of the sixties the space element was introduced more often. The recording studios began to use the effect of echo and reverberation more frequently, imitating the spacious sound quality found in some churches for instance. New Age music has been influenced by musicians who practise meditation and we may hear the quality of vast spaces in some electronic soundscapes and in synthesiser sound carpets. This development was paralleled by a renewed interest in Gregorian Chant, Tibetan singing bowls, gongs, overtone chanting, meditation music and by the creation of new kinds of instruments such as the monochord. It is probably not coincidental that it was in those years that the physical conquest of outer space was given so much attention. Let us remember the film 'Space Odyssey 2000'. The quality of *space* seems to have become universally more important since the sixties.

Working suggestions
Is the person able to listen to others playing ? Can she comment on it ? Is she able to communicate musically with another musician ? If there is a lack of *space* in her music ask which other element(s) do attract our attention and start working with that element.

By emphasising the five elements in musical expression and by using sound paintings rather than melodies, all the participants in a workshop can **meet on the same level**, for in reality are we not all on the same level? In the context of real creativity, of any spiritual development, are we not always beginners in some way or other, whether young or old, musicians or non-musicians, mentally or physically more or less handicapped ? To be creative, to grow, demands of us a readiness to move into the unknown. Courage is needed and a playful or light-hearted approach – *as in music so in life*.

I worked in an institution for handicapped adults for over two years giving weekly music workshops. Some of the staff and the majority of parents were resistant to this and could not see how music would do anything beneficial for these people. It was striking that it was members of the staff who would not participate in playing music. They probably felt more inhibited than the handicapped participants themselves. The handicapped adults though loved it and demonstrated how much these workshops had meant to them when at the final concert in front of parents and friends, every single handicapped participant insisted on coming onto the stage to play. The music workshops had brought out their joy and was for some people a way to reduce the frustration of not being able to make themselves understood because of the lack of appropriate language.

In my courses I often let participants draw what they experience when someone else is playing. The presence or absence of certain elements, the specific forms that an element can take, are always as revealing for the participants as for those who are playing. The players realise how precisely feelings can be expressed and come to appreciate the wealth of information revealed in an improvisation. The five-element approach gives us many keys to understand our psycho-energetic system, our emotions and thought structures, the tensions in our body, our beliefs and our deeper needs. It is always fascinating to see how much of our inner life is accurately reflected in our expression. Thus musicality, inspiration, creativity, luminosity in one's playing become accessible, understandable and are placed in a dynamic that everyone can learn to control.

When working with students, patients or clients it can be very helpful to be aware of when and how they engage with the five elements.

The five elements in Chinese and Tibetan tradition

In traditional Chinese medicine (TCM) one can find very old texts going back to Huang Di, the 'Yellow Emperor' in 600 BCE (Husson, 1973; Paul P. & M., 1983), that recommend the use of specific musical instruments because of their impact on one of the five phases of energy transformation, wood, fire, earth, metal and water. Even though these five phases have similar names to the five elements I work with, and are very often referred to as 'the five elements', they are used differently and do not mean exactly the same thing. They refer to five phases of energy when each element is continually being transformed into the next one in the cycle. 'Wood' in TCM is naturally tending towards 'fire' and 'fire' toward 'earth' and so forth. This system differs from the five-element system used in Ancient Greece, India, Tibet and developed by Paracelsus in Europe. In these systems the five elements represent five levels of densification of energy, going from the most subtle one *ether* to the densest *earth*, the one that corresponds to the physical body. Nevertheless, TCM enables us to better understand the phenomenon of the five elements. There are numerous bridges of understanding between Chinese cosmogony and our own. Since we are all dealing with the same human condition this is hardly extraordinary.

TCM focuses more on the particular element's dynamic connection to the physical organs, the psychosomatic aspect as well as the energy meridians, while the psycho-energetic system focuses more on the different energy fields, especially on the etheric fields and the role of the chakras in the assimilation and distribution of energy. More research is needed to understand how the two systems are connected. Traditional Tibetan medicine has made that connection and has formulated a synthesis between three ancient systems of medicine, Indian, Chinese and Tibetan (Wangyal, 2002).

TCM suggests playing specific music instruments to activate each of the five phases of transformation. For the earth phase they suggest a clay pot into which one can blow to produce a deep sound, an ocarina for example. For the metal phase they suggest tubular bells, for the water phase drums, for the wood phase bamboo flutes and for fire instruments with silk strings are recommended although nowadays these would more likely be carbon fibre strings or gut stringed harps. For earth I sometimes use flower pots with felt mallets and for water a large double-sided Nepalese frame drum. It is interesting to see how the TCM phase of earth corresponds in many ways to the element *earth*, in the psycho-energetic system, especially when it comes to the capacity for concentration. The water organs in TCM, bladder and kidneys, do nicely correspond to our hara chakra. TCM's wood includes the liver and is accordingly in the area influenced by the *fire* region in the solar plexus, while the TCM fire is linked to the heart towards which all energy moves naturally when transformed in the psycho-energetic *fire* area.

The five elements *earth, water, fire, air* and *space* are strongly present in Tibetan tradition, particularly in the Bön tradition of pre-Buddhist times. They use an approach very similar to the psycho-energetic system in that their understanding is strongly influenced by observing how the elements behave in nature. The Tibetans' description of the qualities of the elements is very similar too. Tibetan tradition has also constructed bridges to the Indian ayurvedic tradition. Some Tibetan healing traditions use six chakras (Wangyal, 2002), others use five. Wangyal Rinpoche's approach also makes a bridge to TCM by linking metal with *air*, wood with *fire* and TCM's fire with psycho-energetic's *space*. As often happens, this complementarity can inspire one to go deeper into the subject thus bringing one new understanding.

The Five Elements & their correspondences

	earth	water	fire	air	space
Quality of element	solid	liquid	heat, light, warmth	light, invisible, free, flexible	Emptiness
Body zone	feet > sacrum	> heat point, 3 fingers under navel	> lower end of sternum	chest	> eye brows
Type of energy	masculine	feminine	masculine	feminine	unified
Tendency	descending, adhesive	descending, gathering	ascends, expands, ripens	dispersing	dissolving
Symbol	▢	☽	△	○	⊙
Zodiac sign	♉ ♍ ♑	♓ ♋ ♏	♈ ♌ ♐	♒ ♓ ♎	
Tibetan	gives support	Amalgam-mates	amplifies	allows movement	
Chakra	root	hara	solar plexus	heart	thyroid
Endocrine glands	adrenals	ovaries, testicles	pancreas	thymus	thyroid
Location of chakra	sacrum, at back	5 fingers below navel	stomach	middle of sternum	throat
Reich's bodyzone	buttocks	belly	diaphragm	chest	neck
Sense	smell	taste	sight	touch	hearing
Emotion	insecurity	anger	fear	depression	suppression
Feeling	security	calm	love, under-standing	joy	expression
Quality	stability, con-centration	vitality, creativity	Transformation of emotions	inspiration	essence, emptiness
Level	physique	etheric	astral	mental	conscience
Etheric	life ether	chemical ether	light ether	Reflector ether	

On the Sources of our Inspiration

Improvisation having been a major part of my musical activity for over 40 years now, I wanted to know where our ideas and impulses come from. I asked C how many levels or spheres existed in the spiritual dimension. They willingly said: 21. This led me to explore what these levels were. Then I realized there were also other type of inspirations like mental ones or astral ones. Here as well C immediately told me how many levels there were. This has become a fascinating exploration and brought an understanding how intertwined our worlds are. We get influenced by them and these worlds and beings get influenced by what we do. These impulses come like the impression of a sunset; we are keeping our free will, but are connected to all there is. [5]

The four planes of impulses or inspiration

We are getting our impulses, intuitions and inspirations from lots of different external sources. We may differentiate four main sources: etheric, astral, mental and spiritual planes; each store a different quality, information, memory and may come from various beings; each displaying a specific type of activity. We also find these dimensions around the human body as energy fields (see drawing page 103).

Comparable to a library, the **ETHERIC** stores all our perceptions without discernment: sound, images, tastes, smells and tactile sensations. We find an etheric energy field around humans, animals, plants, stones and nature in general. It is responsible for the entire energy distribution in our body and in the etheric that surrounds it with the help of energy lines (Chinese meridians, Indian nadis, our psychic streams, energy centres like the chakras). The etheric is usually not a source of inspiration, with the exception of inspirations from nature spirits.

The **ASTRAL** contains our emotional & feeling memories, including emotions linked to an event, past or present.

The **MENTAL AURA** or mental energy field contains all our mental activity and stores all the thoughts connected to a particular event in our life. The higher mental plane takes one into dimensions beyond the intellect. In the human aura the higher mental is found above the belief streams in the mental aura; whereas the lower mental, or intellect, is found below the belief streams in the mental aura. The lower mental is far more infiltrated and colored by our emotions and ego.

The **SPIRITUAL AURA** is storing information that can best be described as higher feelings and spiritual qualities. These are different from upper astral feelings like joy, serenity, compassion etc. Once we move our consciousness beyond the known etheric, astral and mental dimensions, the spiritual dimension opens up more fully. Higher feelings allow us to discern what we find in these levels. For example, the essence of an angel is beyond words, thoughts, emotions, 'lower' feelings or sensory perceptions like smell, taste, sound, etc. even if the presence of an angel may sometimes create echoes in those lower layers of consciousness.

The lower astral plane is the area where we find our dead angles, our ego and where intrusive beings can bring 'non-divine impulses' or 'false inspirations'. [5]

The following may be complex to grasp. Yet, when we start seeing more clearly the difference between egoless and ego motivated impulses, we have done already half of what matters here. You can also use the lists with a pendulum or suchlike.

Astral plane   (24 levels)
 1-12 lower astral (painful emotions)
 1 - fear
 2 - dishonesty
 3 - lust, instinctive drive, libido, raw creative power
 4 - anger
 5 - hate
 6 - feelings of inferiority/superiority
 7 - greed
 8 - jealousy, envy, competitiveness
 9 - false pride

10 - sarcasm, cynicism
11 - self pity
12 - sluggishness, self-indulgence, lack of clarity of
motivation

13-24 upper astral (feelings)
13 - success, acceptance of present circumstances &
bases of a situation, 'easy is right' or a naturalness
14 - surrender to the universal or divine intelligence
15 - calmness, serenity, naturalness, humbleness
16 - love, understanding, truth
17 - joy, celebration of life and creation
18 - compassion
19 - faith, trust
20 - ecstasy, delight
21 - unity, softness
22 - freedom of mind and beliefs
23 - knowing, beingness
24 - eternity, harmony, love

Mental plane (32 levels) 1-9 is ego / 10-20 is 'intuition' /
21-32 is inspiration from the divine field

Similar to the astral world, the mental plane can be understood as a separate world existing in another dimension. It can be a source of mental inspiration through concepts, ideas and visions (e.g. sacred geometry). Art can also influence back onto these mental levels. As we can see in the list below there are fundamentally different levels within the mental plane. Level 1-9 are representing the ego level or lower mental. This type of mental activity is fuelled and often heavily tinted by painful emotions; that is the infiltration of emotions into the lower mental aura. We will not be expanding on this here any further [6].

1- 9 linked to ego and emotions
1 - good intentions but lacking awareness of underlying
emotions
2 – limitation of dualistic concepts

3 - wanting to impress others, unbalance between feelings
  and expression
4 - exaggerated, eccentric creativity
5 - ego based intellectual constructs
6 - false ambitions
7 - cultural beliefs
8 - ungrounded ideals
9 - beliefs from erroneous teachings, false authorities

10-12 personal wisdom and experience
10 - of karmic nature
11 - result of cooperation with the non-physical
12 – personal present life wisdom

13-16 ET's information
13 – ET technology
14 – ET energy knowledge
15 – ET wisdom (philosophy, social matters, governance)
16 – ET visions for the future

17-20 light beings and angel information
17 – angel of a nation
18 – energy alignment and balance
19 – thought structures coming from the spirit of time
20 – angel of groups of nations (Europe)
  conceptual level of creation

21-24 inspirational thoughts from archangels on
21 – teachings of personal transformation, bringing light
  into darkness
22 – education, spiritual training
23 – healing, faith, divine will
24 – devotion, service, compassion
25 – spiritual issues taught by principalities
26 – highly evolved spirits like 'C', masters, etc.

27-32 divine inspiration
27 - nature of light
28 - Underlying concepts of harmony

29 - Underlying concepts of beauty
30 - nature of non-duality
31 - nature of love
32 - spirit of evolution, progress and innovation

Higher feeling or spiritual plane   (21 levels)
These levels of higher feelings can only be perceived through the upper two of the three layers of our reflector ether. As we progress in our personal development, we naturally open ourselves to the perception through the reflector ether. (see page 27)

The spiritual plane is a high source of inspiration. A piece of music for example would also reflect back its influence into the spiritual plane. The following list was again elaborated in cooperation with 'C'. Level 17 sees the introduction by 'C' of the ‚**Cupids**'. These are not found in known lists about the hierarchy of angels. 'C' obviously wanted to include them as they are specifically **the high angels of art**. In the roman mythology Cupido is the son of Venus who can transform people with his arrows of love and beauty. Obviously, we are referring to Cupids in a wider sense as they are a high level of angels who are specialized in the spreading of beauty, art and love.

Bear in mind: No matter how much we try to understand the divine dimension, we will only succeed up to a certain degree. Again: the numbering is NOT meant to be a value judgement; it could be replaced by alphabetic letters, colours or symbols.

1   - landscape or area angels
     - Dagdas & Devas*; spirit of time;
2   - individual or group karma
     - creators of form
     - angels of small lakes, rivers* & deserts (Namibian desert angel)
3   - wisdom and experience of nature spirits
     - Kali (breaking down & renewal)
     - angels of larger lakes and rivers

- strato cirrus cloud Angels
- regional angels*
- angels of larger deserts (Gobi & Sahara)
- the 72 angels
4 - inspirations from shamanic light beings
- Indonesian tropical forest angel
- some non-intrusive ET's*
5 - Sophia (wisdom)
- life force; wisdom of animals
- angels of large tropical forests (Amazonian, equatorial African)
6 - nation angels*: art inspired by them and which
contributes to shape the spirit of a nation
7 - angel or spirit of a continent*: Europe, Middle East,
North America, Arica, etc.
8 - respect for life and creation
- angel of science, knowledge & education
- friendly ET's like those from Pegasus*
- underlying structures of life
- ocean angels: Atlantic, Pacific, etc.,
- smaller mountain range: Pyrenees, Appalachians
9 - St. Bridget - Goddess of Spring and Poetry
- the major Elementals (earth, water, fire, air), volcanoes
- larger mountain range angels: Ural, Himalaya,
Alps, Andes, Rocky Mountains, etc.
10 - planet Earth angel*
11 - church angels* : protecting altars, statues, crucifix, etc.,
- Archangels*: Prayer/Sound (Sandalphon); good news &
creativity (Gabriel); hope & aspiration (Ramiel); service
(Jehudiel); faith & spiritual strength (Saraquiel); justice &
harmony (Raguel); wisdom (Raziel); transformation of the
shadow (Binael); of healing (Raphael); teaching (Uriel),
Light into shadow (Michael); Divine will (Hesediel)
12 - Archai – Lordships, Principalities – leading the earth
leaders, people and communities
13 - Kyriotetes : instructing the duties of the angels below them);
their energy is pure grace;

- Transmission of the Teachings of Christ
- teachings of aliveness
- Ignacio de Loyola*, Franz of Assisi, Theresa of Avila, St. Hildegard, St. Cecilia, etc.
14 - Exusiai - Powers : protecting the heavenly spheres from all negative influences of the earthly spheres. Keep the world in balance and especially the balance with the dark forces.
15 - Dynameis - Virtues : directing the cycles of the planets; celestial harmony
16 - Dominions : leading the angels of the earth, of continents and nations
17 - Cupids : Arts, love and beauty
18 - Thrones : angels or spirits of divine will and life energy, giving impulses of direction for humanity
19 - Cherubim : angels or spirits of harmony and wisdom
20 - Seraphim : angels or spirits of light & fire, igniters
21 - Black Madonna*, Christ, Creator, Holy Spirit, Buddha, etc.

*) I have expanded on devas, landscape and area angels, angels of nations, the whole spectrum of non-physical beings, the human aura, layers of the soul, in "Faith is the Bridge" [6].

(source: 'C', www.engelwelt.de and other webpages on this theme of angel hierarchies)

My list of angels does not correspond to what you may find on internet. In the 1st and 6th century Dionysius Areopagita (and his reincarnation) established a list of nine types of angels and their hierarchy, but mentioned that that list was only an approximate model and that the only one who would know the exact facts was the Creator himself. 'C' introduced the 'Cupids' and insisted that the 'Dominions' were not the same as the Kyriotetes (Greek word). The Dominions have, according to 'C', their own list of tasks as mentioned above; thus bringing the list of levels of angels to 11.

We must never forget: the feelings we experience in contemplating a work of art are the most important – and feelings always contain a part of mystery. When we have a real interest in a question and carry it with us it will bring maturation over time.

You can say that the angels from level 17-20 are the '**rulers**', from 12-16 the '**administrators**' and those form level 1-11 are the '**transmitters**', those who have contacts with humans. In elaborating this list, I have included a large number of angels that care for areas in nature: deserts, tropical forests, nations, lakes, etc. As we all live in some 'area' or other we are part of and may feel the particular type of landscape angel taking care of it. Some artistic inspirations are naturally coming in that way. You may call it 'the beauty of a valley' or '..of a lake', '..of a particular mountain area', 'the spirit of a place' etc.

turkish
1312131

7 Types of conceptualization in music, etc.

Each type has its function. None is 'better' than another.
There are intermediary forms to be explored as well.

1. physical material manifestation of buildings, trees, hills, etc.
   In Music: unshaped primordial physical sound
2. etheric the raw sounds in the alphabet
   In Music: Transepulsations and –syllables, continuous
   drone sounds, work songs (slaves, sailors, waulking
   Songs of the Hebrides), walking blues
3. level 3 the shaped sounds of our alphabet: A, B, C, etc.
   In Music: Melodic, 3-4 -chords, mainly 4 beats, festive
   dance - and Pop music, most classical music, etc.
4. level 4 Egyptian Hieroglyphs, Pictograms, Chinese Ideograms,
   In Music: multilayered compositions with
   simultaneous variety of chord sequences, rhythms,
   melody aspects; Alban Berg, most Jazz after 1965, etc.
5. level 5 primal symbols of energy: □ △ + –– • ○
   In Music: free Improvisations, no continuous
   rhythm, nor repetitive sequence of chords nor Melodies;
   highly complex and feeling music, giving life to the
   space between two notes.
   e.g. Aulos scale (undertone scale)
6. level 6 *In Music*: free floating, felt sounds, toning
7. divine *In Music*: music of the spheres, we cannot reach

According to the think tank D the level of spiritual energy in distant healing with the harp potentially trebles from one level to the next. This concerns the energy that spreads through the reflector ether when playing for distant healing (as seen on the map page 28) and happens especially when feeling and a higher awareness are involved in playing.

Other tonal systems, a brief overview

My path in exploring Music & Energy has led me to search for limitations in our playing. I needed to make sure there were no hidden limitations that would inhibit what musical expression could do at its best. Our tonal system, as found on the piano e.g., is of course just one way of organizing musical notes. Having looked extensively into different kinds of folk music from around the world, I came across Balinese gamelan music and its unique pentatonic slendro scale. These five notes are not part of our 12 notes and induce quite a different way of playing, having almost an inherently different type of rhythmical feature. This made me see that other types of musical systems invariably bring about or are created by a totally different way of thinking.

You find this also in the **Aulos scale**, an undertone scale that is also called the Schlesinger Scale after the British archeologist who found flutes in an archeological site in Greece at the beginning of 20th century. *The Greek Aulos*, London: Methuen, 1939. Downloadable for free on Open Library

I have been fascinated by this tonal system for over 35 years now. It brings a totally different way of thinking music. You cannot play melodies or chords as in our usual well temperate system. You need to play and listen to this scale with a total feeling attention, almost note by note. I have made recordings with my Egyptian bow harp available on danielperret.bandcamp.com

More common is the **overtone scale**, also using eight notes like the Aulos scale. The Aulos scale is actually an exact mirroring of the overtone scale, thus also called the undertone scale.

The so-called '**solfeggio' scale** is another tonal system. I have used it for compositions on 'Sounds like Heaven'.

These other tonal systems make you think outside of the box and force you connect more to feelings. I have often used **flower pots** with their unique musical scales. They are one of the best ways of learning to improvise.

A brief introduction to subtle energy fields

I would like to explain how the sounds of the harp travel and affect the subtle energy fields of the receiving person. For this purpose, we need to have a minimal understanding of the etheric energy field and the function of its main layers. This may appear somewhat complicated and you can of course skip this passage. But should you want to understand how distant healing and prayer function, you need to get a sense of the complexity of the etheric energy fields, which in themselves are a wonder of creation. The essential may lie in understanding the upper layer of the reflector ether. Understanding how energy and spirit work is complex and takes many years of study. This especially concerns this layer of the reflector ether that I explain in more detail further down. Bob Moore said: "The reflector ether is the highest ether, the most advanced contact we can reach with energy." It is in this layer that I am shown the spreading effect of distant healing with the harp. The etheric energy field is NOT part of the known conventional range of electromagnetic frequencies.

The mind, through the third eye/pineal chakra, directs the energy to a receiver by using their name, photo, or geographic location. The upper reflector ether is the media through which the energy flows. It reaches the receiver in their upper reflector ether. From there it moves down into the other layers of the etheric and into their spiritual aura. From there it would move into the other layers of the aura, above all into the upper mental aura, the upper astral aura.

It is best to see the conventional range of electromagnetic frequencies as only one kind of waves, let's say 'vertical waves.' There exist a number of other worlds with their particular types of energy and organization of frequencies. C suggests for example that love energy is a spiral, that spiritual energies have horizontal waves, astral and etheric energies have two possible diagonal patterns, whereas mental energies travel in information packages (no waves at all). The etheric in general is made up of over 50'000 levels or diagonal frequencies.

The human etheric is made up of only 4 levels of the etheric, organized in sub layers, each one having its specific function. Plants, animals also have the same four ethers: *chemical ether, light ether, life ether* (two sublayers)*, reflector or warmth ether* (three sublayers).
I am repeating here two quotes from texts above:

"**The reflector or warmth ether** contains the feeling between people, it contains world memory, knowledge, wisdom, including physical memory, intuitions. Thoughts enter here before entering the brain. The reflector ether is the highest ether, the most advanced contact we can reach with energy. In this contact with energy you have all the things that are necessary: peace, contentment with yourself, you have the connection with the universe … and finally you have the balance between nature and yourself. The reflector ether is the combination of all of this, but essentially centered around peace." (Bob Moore)

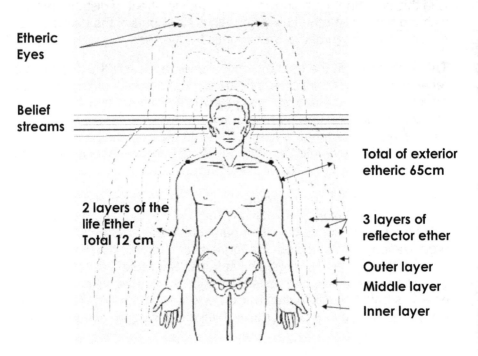

Etheric Eyes

Belief streams

Total of exterior etheric 65cm

2 layers of the life Ether Total 12 cm

3 layers of reflector ether

Outer layer
Middle layer
Inner layer

"Everything that is taking place can be reflected outward. So, you can use the outer part of the etheric as a means of reflecting out emotion (anger or suchlike) or creating your own projections. That is being done from what you would be retaining within yourself, related to your emotions. There is not necessarily a feed in - to reach that - from a higher level. Maybe you are just projecting out again your own reflections back from other people's emotions. That may mean you are separating the outer layer of the etheric from other layers. So, you are just using the outer layer as a reflector backward from what other people are saying to you. You don't want to be hurt so you just throw it back to them again. You are creating a sort of a vicious circle. But that of course is not helpful to the etheric itself nor to the other levels of the etheric which need to be incorporated if you are going to be using say such things as compassion, which is also a reflector."

The lower life ether, that is the layer closest to the skin surface, is in my understanding specialised in facilitating the communication or exchange with the light ether under the skin. This is crucial as there is often a separation operating between those two layers due to a lack of understanding, lack of honesty in feeling and expressing how we feel. If we do not allow what life brings us to 'go under our skin' and if we do not express how we feel about the events of our life and hide our true feelings this creates the separation of the layers. Our five senses function within this layer of the life ether. The memory of their perception is then stored in the upper life ether.

The upper life ether seems to have the task of storing the memory of all our sense impressions: sounds, words, smells, pictures, sceneries, touch, tastes. This is one of the major functions of the etheric: the indiscriminate storing of all we ever perceive. After death it seems that we recall these memories and see them pass by like a film of our life, thus remembering all we did and said. This will help us to learn from our errors. The 'skin' of the upper life ether contains the etheric web, which protects us from uncontrolled astral influences. This web can be damaged by the use of drugs, that can create large holes in the web and thus leave the person very vulnerable to outside influences.

The three etheric layers inside the body
The **Light ether** is just below the skin.
Bob Moore: "The light ether connects to universal structures. It is the means to keep us physically alive. It is reflecting upwards. Light of course is something that is necessary and essential to have drawn into a state where there is for example depression." It also links to truth and honesty. It is the honest part in us, how we truly feel. It connects with the energy of the Holy Ghost, of Love, Truth and Light.

The **chemical ether** (also called sound ether or ether of numbers) is in charge of bringing the prana energy to the cells of the body. It has a strong connection to water, sound, numbers and the symbol of the chemical ether being a half circle. The link to the table of chemical elements seems evident here (scheme of Mendeleiev). This ether seems to be responsible for nourishing the cells, the blood and the bones. The chemical ether is dependent on the good functioning of the three other layers of the etheric. If this blend between the four layers is interrupted or weakened, then the chemical ether cannot nourish the body as it should.

Bob Moore: "**The chemical ether** is strongly connected to metabolism and the removal of waste energy. It is more predominant in the bottom area of the body because of the importance of this part in cleansing waste energy, removing waste from digestion, menstruation, etc."

Higher feelings of the spiritual plane (with its 21 levels) can only be perceived through the upper two of the three layers of our reflector ether [8]. As we progress in our personal development, we naturally open ourselves to these perceptions through the reflector ether.

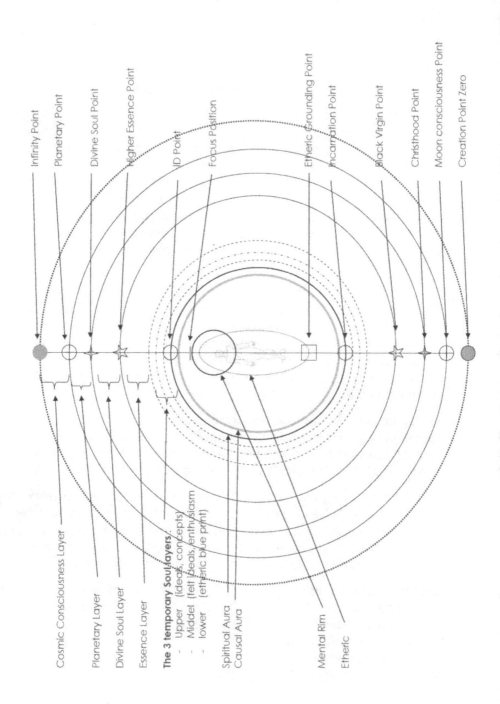

Infinity Point
Planetary Point
Divine Soul Point
Higher Essence Point
ID Point
Focus Position
Etheric Grounding Point
Incarnation Point
Black Virgin Point
Christhood Point
Moon consciousness Point
Creation Point Zero

Cosmic Consciousness Layer
Planetary Layer
Divine Soul Layer
Essence Layer

The 3 temporary Soul layers:
- Upper (ideas, concepts)
- Middel (felt ideals, enthusiasm
- lower (etheric blue print)

Spiritual Aura
Causal Aura

Mental Rim
Etheric

Daniel Perret – The Harp in Distant Healing

Four pillars of personal development

Working with subtle energies in our harp playing depends on an inner work and on reaching higher levels of consciousness. Essentially it is about attracting, connecting with and cooperating with light beings. I have been teaching personal development for forty years and have always been concerned about how one achieves progress and goes beyond inner limits. The answer may be largely individual. Many paths or techniques of development are often elaborate but have a limited success. People are led some distance but then the path does not take them further because of a dead angle inherent to the path. You can see that for example with some people who meditate.

Meditation is a wonderful tool to learn how to quieten the 'inner radio'. Yet, alone it may not allow you to work thoroughly on your shadow, your traumas, neurotic patterns and deep emotional issues. People may meditate for decades and then discover that they have avoided shadow aspects in themselves. It can, by then have become increasingly difficult to start dealing with them, because of age or ingrained habits.

The same goes for **devotional practices** such as prayer. Some people pray wholeheartedly for most of their lives and may also avoid inner shadow work. You can find variations of these limiting patterns, and having a teacher who is aware of these traps is helpful.

People who have gone through **disciplined transformation work** may discover that they have avoided the devotional aspect because they did not look at the resistance they had towards the Christian church for instance. You may become quite a stern, disciplined person doing awareness exercises yet forget to enjoy life and relationships.

Another, common dead angle is the limitations in expression especially of feelings. You can do many years of meditation, devotional work and transformation exercises. Yet if you avoid expressing your inner feelings and emotions, you do not open the thyroid chakra enough. This limits your access to the upper two chakras, the pineal and the crown and the divine field above them.

Until the contrary is being proven, I am in favour of using four pillars in development: meditation (third eye and crown chakras), transformational exercises (root, hara, solar plexus chakras), devotional practices (heart chakra) and spontaneous expression (thyroid chakra). The analogy with the chakras is not the whole story but gives an idea.

Some people can practice **spontaneous artistic expression** for years (painting, music, dance, etc) and may get caught in an unfeeling, eccentric artistic work that does not progress towards upliftment. I have written extensively about this in other books. I cannot describe this in a few sentences here. I believe that the complementarity of these four pillars is useful and not to be overlooked.

I see life as a permanent state of growth and discovery and perceive **three ongoing areas** to work on the first of which is exploring our physical incarnation (transforming the three lower chakras). This means sinking into our own energy fields towards the earth and leads to what I call a connection to the Black Virgin space of Mother Earth. The second is expanding the heart chakra through deepening our empathy and connection to other sentient beings. The third is a permanent expansion into higher and higher, or deeper and deeper (if you prefer) aspects of the divine field, the universe, the unified field, whatever you want to call it. This can be experienced as a connection to the energy above our heads.

melodic minor
2122221

Raising your own vibration
and attracting light beings

Personal development is more precisely spiritual development and is by definition a continuous rising of our consciousness onto higher and finer levels of vibration. This can be compared to the discipline of Zen archery, bee keeping, successful gardening, relating with love to ourselves and to the people or animals we meet.

This process naturally attracts events, situations and the beings we need to help us grow further. This is cared for by our timeless soul, our guardian angel and spirit beings in general. Any forced ambition on our side will only slow down our vibration and the process. We simply need to stay clear in our motivation as to why we do, think and say what we do. Light beings come to us when we are ready and not before, no matter what we do.

I have mentioned the two kinds of concentric energy fields around a harp. When the first few rings show up, we know the harpist can send distant healing to nature spirits. When the second type of rings appear, the mental and the Seraphim field, the harpist is ready to send distant healing to humans and animals. We must humbly take this as steps on our path and trust that the first phase brings invaluable understanding necessary to function on the second level of healing. All forcing comes from the ego and brings nothing other than illusions.

Distant Healing with our harp is a path of learning just as life is. Personal development techniques show how to go about it. We need to focus our attention on the three lower chakras to begin with. Buddhism rightly speaks of five hindrances or main obstacles:

1. Sensual Desire – seeking happiness through the 5 senses
2. Ill-Will – opposite of good will. Resentment, bitterness, hostility, hatred, etc.
3. Sloth and Torpor – laziness of mind
4. Restlessness and Worry - the inability to calm the mind
5. Doubt – lack of conviction or trust

Pineal chakra and its 96 segments

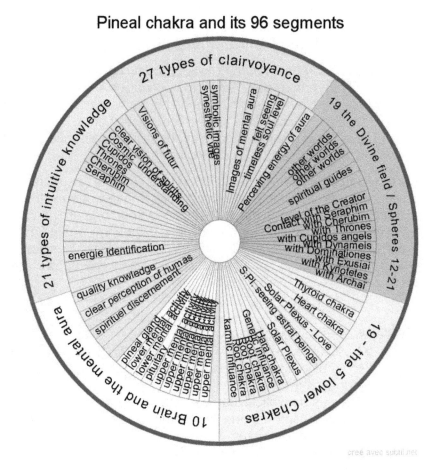

Biography

I was born in Zürich and lived there for forty years. I moved with my family to South-West France, where my wife and I teach and enjoy the area. I began playing music when I was 18, exploring folk traditions from America, UK and Ireland. I played Irish traditional music for 30 years, mainly Uilleann pipes and whistles. I met Bob Moore a spiritual healer from Northern Ireland in 1979 and my wife and I studied with him for 20 years. He taught me so much about development, energy fields and the effects of sound.

I bought a concert pedal harp in 1980, a Celtic harp some years later and recently had an ancient Egyptian bow harp made by a gifted local craftsman. I play feeling improvisations on the harps. That is idiom-free with no rhythms, no melodies and no repetitive chords. My playing aims to give the listener as much freedom as possible, and not catch their mind and endlessly churn in their heads.

My own personal development work has led me not to separate physical and non-physical levels in my life. I have written extensively about energy and energy fields. I have been part of a group of healers practicing distant healing for many years. Although I worked as a music therapist for 14 years in a children's day clinic at Brive Hospital (Central France), I am not a harp therapist, as this requires a specific training.

My books :
1. 'Music – the feeling Way'* (also in French, German and Danish)*
2. 'Roots of Musicality', Jessica Kingsley publishers (also in German & French*)
3. 'Music as a mystical journey'[1] (also in French and Danish) [1]
4. 'Sound healing with the five Elements' Binkey Kok (also in French and German)*
5. 'Creating divine Art – On the Origins of Inspiration' [1] (also in French)
6. 'Faith is the Bridge', BoD [1]
7. 'Guérir la Terre – coopérer avec les forces subtiles de la planète'[1] (also in German)[1]

[1] books published by BoD - Books on Demand, available best through my website in the BoD French library or elsewise over Amazon /
*Downloadable for free on my website

danielperret.bandcamp.com   *www.vallonperret.com*

CPSIA information can be obtained
at www.ICGtesting.com
Printed in the USA
LVHW081352240720
661198LV00010B/316